A Disquisition On The Scene, Origin, Date, Etc., Etc., Of Shakespeare's Tempest

Joseph Hunter

A DISQUISITION

ON

THE SCENE, ORIGIN, DATE,

ETC. ETC.

OF

SHAKESPEARE'S TEMPEST.

IN

A LETTER TO BENJAMIN HEYWOOD BRIGHT, ESQ.

FROM

THE REV. JOSEPH HUNTER, F.S.A.

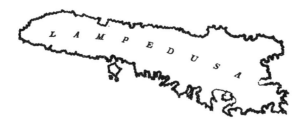

LONDON:

PRINTED BY C. WHITTINGHAM.

1839.

" As these things have never, I believe, been adequately conceived, or systematically discussed, I may perhaps be permitted, on this occasion, to adopt the language of science, and to assume the merit of DISCOVERY. The reader will, at least, be instructed in a portion of knowledge which was before hidden from his view, however he may finally appreciate the importance of the subject, or the dexterity of the teacher."

A Specimen of a Commentary on Shakespeare, by WALTER WHITER.

[ONE HUNDRED COPIES ONLY PRINTED.]

CONTENTS.

I.

INTRODUCTORY.—THE BERMUDAS.

DEAR SIR,

IT is now nearly two years, since at the close of a book of antiquarian literature, I announced, in the accustomed phrase, as ' speedily to be published,' a work to be entitled NEW ILLUSTRATIONS OF THE LIFE, STUDIES, AND WRITINGS OF SHAKESPEARE. The announcement excited some attention. Illustrations of an author on whom the spirit of criticism may seem long ago to have exhausted itself, which are new, and at the same time of any worth, are not of every-day occurrence. The title, I own, was somewhat ambitious; and this makes me feel that I am brought under a kind of obligation, if not to account for the delay, and possibly the non-appearance of the work, to give the public the means of judging whether I was prepared to execute what I had taken upon myself voluntarily to announce.

As the best way in which this can be done, I shall print what I proposed to say on THE TEMPEST, the first play which presents itself, for I follow the old and accustomed arrangement, which I could never see any sufficient reason for changing. As for the reasons of the delay, let it be enough that I had

B

reckoned without my host, the booksellers. I give these Illustrations as a *Specimen* of what my work would have been, just as Johnson gave his notes on *Macbeth* as a specimen of his intended annotation on the whole of the plays. I do not, however, mean to say, that I have matter equally new and equally important to present on every other play as on this. On two or three of the plays it may be that I have been equally fortunate in the discoveries which I have made respecting them : but many of them afford very little scope for discovery, and nearly all the annotation that is necessary or proper is already done for them. I must confess that, as concerns this design, it was fortunate for me that *The Tempest* did occupy the first place, on account of what I regard the very great misapprehensions which are entertained concerning it.

The plan on which I have proceeded is this : to give first such remarks as I have to make on each play considered as a whole : and then remarks on particular scenes or passages. But instead of printing what I have to say upon *The Tempest* as it was originally written, I shall throw my materials into the form of a regular Disquisition : and I shall copy Dr. Farmer, whose Essay on the Learning is in the form of a letter to a Shakespearian friend, but with this difference (would that it were the only difference), that while his letter proceeds as letters should do, in unbroken continuity, I shall divide mine into sections. This is contrary to rule, but I prefer this plan to a series of letters ; and who can tell, as Dr. Farmer asks, whether it may not one day be demonstrated that a departure from rule is peculiarly happy when the subject is Shakespeare ?

If I were asked why of all my friends I address myself to you, I might reply, that I know no one who goes beyond you in zeal for the honour of this great Poet, or who takes a deeper interest in those minute and curious questions, so many of which arise whenever the mind is directed on these wonderful works, in the true spirit of critical research. In you also I recognize one to whom all that has been already done for Shakespeare is perfectly familiar, and who can therefore distinguish between those observations which are new, and which really advance our knowledge of this author and his works, and those which are the mere repetition of what has long ago been remarked. To your justice also, as well as to your discrimination, I dare commit myself. But I have another reason. This is no new subject of communication between us. In those pleasant Shakespearian conversations which your retirement into the country has now interrupted, I have more than once drawn your attention to the arguments by which certain very important conclusions concerning this play are supposed to have been fully established. We have agreed concerning their insufficiency. But when I would have substituted for them other arguments leading to far different conclusions, I have not been so fortunate as to obtain your concurrence. To what must I attribute this? I cannot attribute it to the weakness of the arguments, because I think them sufficient to enforce assent. I am, therefore, thrown on the imperfect manner in which they have been exhibited; and, indeed, you have seen them but in parts and parcels, and never in one view with all the connections and dependencies. You will regard me. therefore, now, if you will allow me so to speak, as

returning to the attack. I mean to set the whole
argument in due form before you. It is an *experi-
mentum crucis*. If I now fail to convince you that
the island of Prospero is at last discovered, and that
when Shakespeare began this play, he had not *Jourdan's pamphlet* before him, but a *far worthier work*,
I must suppose myself the sport of some such mischievous spirit as Ariel, and nothing will remain for
me but to retire from the scene, like Prospero himself,
breaking my staff and drowning my unhappy book.
I do not propose to rest even here. I have other new
and curious views to unfold; not, I am persuaded,
airy unreal visions, such as deluded the senses of
Alonzo and his companions, but real substantial truths.
Perhaps I may shew you an archetype of Caliban,
who is generally supposed to be a creature wholly of
Shakespeare's imagination. I do not even despair of
succeeding in a still bolder part of my undertaking,
and convincing you, in opposition to the whole body
of critics and commentators, that *The Tempest*, instead of being the latest work of this great master, is
in reality one of the earliest, nearly the first in time,
as the first in place, of the dramas which are wholly
his. The other conclusions are of great importance
in the criticism of this one play, but the last is important in the history of the Poet's mind, studies,
and genius.

You know with how much skill and labour the
argument has been wrought out by which the date
of this play is supposed to be established. You
remember how much is said by Mr. Malone in his
Essay on the Chronological Order, * and how much

* Boswell's Malone, 8vo. 1821, vol. ii. p. 464.

more by Mr. Chalmers in his review of that Essay. †
You also know that beside dealing with this play as
they deal with the rest in their general investigations
of the chronology of these writings, that both Mr.
Malone and Mr. Chalmers wrote and printed express
Dissertations on this subject, ‡ in which the question
is again handled, and the argument exhibited with
more minuteness in the details. The question,
therefore, may at least be considered, *dignus vindice*
by authority. These two eminent critics usually write,
as critics are wont, with an air of confidence, but
their conviction seems more decided on this point than
on almost any other arising in this branch of Shakespeare commentatorship. You also know that, differ-
ing as they did on so many other points, on this they
were so far agreed, that both supposed that the play
must have been written after the year 1610, Mr.
Malone assigning it to 1611, and Mr. Chalmers to
1613. Both placed the composition of it after 1610
for the same reason, namely, that there is throughout
allusion to the wreck of two Englishmen, Sir George
Somers and Sir Thomas Gates, in the Bermudean
seas, an event which happened in 1609; and even

---

† *A Supplementary Apology for the Believers*, 8vo. 1799,
p. 438.

‡ Mr. Malone's Dissertation is printed in the 15th volume of
the edition of Shakespeare, known by the name of Boswell's Malone, p. 377—434. Mr. Chalmers' Dissertation is a tract which
was circulated among his private friends, and which has not, I
believe, been published. He has also much on this question in ·
An Apology for the Believers, 8vo. 1797, p. 577, *et seq.* Theobald had before them asserted that this play could not have been
written before the Bermudas was discovered, in which he is right:
but when he adds that the discovery was in 1609, the year of
Somers' shipwreck, he shews a want of acquaintance with the progress of maritime discovery.

special allusions to passages in a narrative of that shipwreck, which was printed in 1610. I pass over as undeserving of notice other writers who have touched on this question, because I cannot find that any of them has done more than repeat what the two critics, whom I have named, have told us. For one original enquirer, we have twenty persons who write what before has been written without any enquiry at all.

You have then now before you the main argument for the late date assigned to this play. Accessory or corroborative evidence there is none worth regarding. I shall throw it into a syllogism. When Shakespeare wrote *The Tempest*, he had in view the tempest in which Somers and Gates were wrecked on the Bermudas : that tempest occurred in 1609; *argal*, as the grave-digger has it, the play must have been written in or after that year.

Nothing can be more conclusive. But what if some one were to step in and deny the major? If any one should succeed in persuading the public that not the real storm in which Somers and Gates were wrecked, but a storm the invention of a great poet, great almost as Shakespeare, was in Shakespeare's mind when he wrote the early scenes of this play, and that not the Bermudas, but an island in far other seas is the archetype of the island of Prospero, we shall no longer be obliged to assign this play to a time subsequent to the tempest of 1609, but shall be at liberty to place it at such a period of the Poet's life as from other considerations we may be led to conclude concerning it.

Was then the storm of 1609 in the Poet's mind; and did the island of Bermuda suggest to him either the general idea of a small and deserted island in a stormy sea, subject to enchantment, or any of the particular circumstances of the isle of Prospero? I shall invert the order, and take the second of these questions first.

And here I know that the words of Ariel will immediately occur to you, and to all who read this Disquisition,

> " in the deep nook, where once
> Thou call'dst me up at midnight, to fetch dew
> From the still-vex'd Bermoothes :"   *Act* i. *Sc.* 2.

which are proof indisputable that the mind of the Poet was once at least directed on this island as he wrote the play, and on the stormy character of the seas by which it is surrounded. But when I have admitted this, I have admitted all that can justly be inferred from this passage, if it can be shewn that Bermuda was an island infamous for storms and the danger of the navigation of the seas around it, long before those circumstances were made more the subject of conversation by the lamentable event which occurred in 1609.

For proof that this was the case, I must own myself in part indebted to the older commentators, who, for another purpose, have collected some of the notices of the island from voyagers who wrote before the time when Sil. Jourdan (I give all that is known of his name) published his narrative of the shipwreck of Somers and Gates. An account was printed of a shipwreck suffered by one Henry May in those seas, who arrived in England in August 1594, after having been for five months on the island building the vessel in which he returned home. Sir Robert Dudley, the enterprising and ingenious son

of the Earl of Leicester, who returned to England
from a voyage in May 1595, had directed his course
towards the Bermudas, hoping to find there the
Havanna fleet dispersed: " the fleet," says he, " I
found not, but foul weather enough to scatter many
fleets." The narratives of both these navigators are
in Hackluyt. And finally, there is a passage in Sir
Walter Raleigh's *Discovery of Guiana*, printed in
1596, which is of itself quite sufficient to shew that
Shakespeare might easily be acquainted with the
stormy character of those seas long before it was
forced on public observation, by the incident to which
allusion has so often been made, and which, for
reasons afterwards to be given, is probably the true
origin of the slight reference to the Bermudas in this
play ; " the rest of the Indies for calms and diseases
very troublesome, and the Bermudas a hellish sea
for thunder, lightning and storms."

We see, then, that there is not the least occasion
to go to a tract printed in 1610, for the knowledge
which Shakespeare evidently possessed of the island
of Bermuda and its perpetual storms; and the
utmost that can, with any appearance of probability,
be said of this passage is, that the introduction of
" the still-vex'd Bermoothes," may possibly be one
of those oblique allusions in which the genius of
Shakespeare so much delighted, in which he half
discloses a truth, or leads the mind to a particular
train of thought without appearing to do so.

That he does thus indirectly insinuate a meaning,
and give in a distant, and perhaps ambiguous phrase,
a key to what is a main purpose of his work, no one
will doubt, who has studied these remarkable compositions with close attention. But supposing that

in the expression " the still-vex'd Bermoothes," we were to recognize one of those obscure and indirect intimations, we ought, when the hint is taken, and we have transported ourselves to the island itself, to find resemblances which are direct and unequivocal. If in this we fail, the supposition that we possess a reference that is oblique, is not only gratuitous but unreasonable.

And especially when we find that the idea of a stormy sea was so associated with the idea of the Bermudas, in the minds of the poets contemporary with Shakespeare, that this island is for ever being intruded upon us when storms and tempests are their theme. I shall not cite honest John Taylor for this purpose, though his writings may be used much more than they have yet been used, for the illustration of Shakespeare; or Drayton's notice of the Bermudas in that strange medley, *The Odcombian Banquet;* but take you at once to Sir Fulk Grevile, who was residing at his castle at Warwick, when Shakespeare was living, first, or nearly the first of the aristocracy of the neighbouring town of Stratford :

" Whoever sails near to Bermuda coast
Goes hard aboard the monarchy of Fear,
Where all desires, but life's desire, are lost,
For wealth and fame put off their glories there.
Yet this isle, poison-like, by mischief known,
Weans not desire from her sweet nurse, the sea ;
But, unseen, shews us where our hopes be sown,
With woeful signs declaring joyful way.
For who will seek the wealth of western sun,
Oft by Bermuda's miseries must run."
CÆLICA, Sonnet lviii.*

* Possibly this may be taken as a proof also, that the Bermudas was familiarly known in England not only before the loss of Somers' ship, but before the return of Raleigh from his first voy-

When Chapman, in his *Epicede or Funeral Song*, on the death of Prince Henry, 1612, introduces a storm at sea, it is the storm in which Sir Thomas Gates was cast on the Bermudas;

> " when not a tear-wrack'd eye
> Could tell in all that dead time, if they were
> Sinking or sailing; till a quickning clear
> Gave light to save them by the ruth of rocks
> At the Bermudas, where the tearing shocks
> And all the miseries before, more felt
> Than here half-told" -   -   -

I must not go on; neither Grevile nor Chapman pleases, often as we have been told to admire, especially the latter : and I shall give you a prose testimony which is worth them both:

> " Navigators report that there is a sea in the voyage to the West Indies (called the Bermudas) which is a most hellish sea for thunder, lightning and storms.   Also they assure us of an island which they call the Island of Devils ; for to such as approach near the same, there do not only appear fearful sights of devils and evil spirits, but also mighty tempests with most terrible and continual thunder and lightning ; and the noise of horrible cries, with screeching, doth so affright and amaze those that come near that place, that they are glad, with all might and main, to fly and speed them thence with all possible haste they can;—"

with which Thomas Tymme, from whose *Silver Watch Bell* I have quoted, connects some pleasant moralization.   The book was exceedingly popular, as I quote from the tenth edition, published in 1614.

These references to the Bermudas have been quoted

---

age, for the *Cælica* is one of *Certain learned and elegant works of the Right Honourable Fulk Lord Brooke, written in his youth, and familiar exercise with Sir Philip Sidney*, folio 1633, while Sir Philip Sidney died in 1586.   The two friends had entered the Grammar School of Shrewsbury on the same day, October 17, 1564, on which day, Sir James Harington, cousin to Sir Philip, was also entered, as appears by the book of entrances which is kept there.

or referred to, for the purpose of shewing that the
topic was a familiar one with the poets and miscel-
laneous writers of the time, and that therefore when
we find Shakespeare speaking, as he does, of " the
still-vex'd Bermoothes," there is no reason to suspect
him of having any obscure, oblique, indirect, or concealed allusion or intention; anything, in short, but
what the words naturally convey. The Bermudas
was in fact a common-place of the time.

We come then next to inquire, whether in the
details of the reports concerning this island of the
far Atlantic, there is such a conformity with the
image which Shakespeare presents before us of the
island on which he has placed Prospero and Miranda,
that when once the resemblance has been suggested,
we acknowledge it to exist, and are led to the inference, that when the Poet delineated it he thought
of the peculiar characters with which the island of
Bermuda is invested. This is the position taken by
Mr. Malone and Mr. Chalmers; and for the details
they rely principally on the statements in the pamphlet of Jourdan.

Here, then, is a case of literary resemblance, or
rather, literary suggestion; and before I proceed, I
must draw your attention to a well known canon in
comparative criticism. Imitation or suggestion is
not to be inferred from coincidence in circumstances
which are obvious and familiar; but only when, *first*,
this coincidence extends to a great number of such
circumstances, to the almost entire exclusion of any
other; *second*, when it is found in the case of circumstances which lie remote from observation, or
which are rarely, if ever, introduced by other writers
when describing events of the same kind; and *third*,

when there is coincidence of a striking character in the words or phrases in which the real event, or the image in the mind of a poet delineating an imaginary scene, is represented.

Thus any poet may form in his mind an image of an island, without a human being to pace the ground or to awaken its echoes; he may place it where the surges of the sea are for ever chafing against its rock-bound coast, and on the hidden rocks more fatal to the mariner; he may even make the solitude and the danger more awful, by placing it under the peculiar presidency of some dimly-discovered and unreal being: and if it were proved that the same conception had long before been formed in the mind of some other poet, or if there were notice of such an island in some book of navigations, it would still, if there were nothing more, be an unreasonable presumption that the one *suggested* the other. I am not in this enquiry concerned with that kind of imitation which is called plagiarism, in which there is some kind of corrupt appropriation of the ideas or expressions of an earlier writer; but it may be observed, that if from the kind of resemblance of which I have spoken, such kind of imitation is inferred, the censure would be most unjust. And as there are numerous circumstances which are *obvious* and *necessary* adjuncts to such a conception as that which I have described, so obvious and so necessary that they must arise in any mind of any fertility, so many of these circumstances may co-exist in two distinct literary compositions, and there be no connexion of imitation or suggestion between them. The same may be said of a storm at sea. It is nothing in proof of imitation or suggestion, if we find the violence of the wind, the tearing of the sails, the breaking of the mast, the loss of the rudder, the striking on a rock, the mastery of the waves, the exertions of the mariners, the steady courage of the captain, and the distress of the passengers. These things are but the ordinary accompaniments of a storm. They are found whenever a storm at sea is described in verse or in prose. The greatest and the meanest poets have them : Virgil and Aldhelm. There must be something more than this; some less prominent circumstance, something which not every mind would be disposed to select from the many adjuncts of a storm, and think it fitted for the purposes of poetry, some coincidence in an unusual form of expression, or, at least, a coincidence in the selection of ordinary circumstances which shall extend through nearly the whole range, before we are justly warranted in inferring that the earlier description *suggested* the later.

Now apply this very just and reasonable canon to the image which Shakespeare has delineated of the island of Prospero, as compared with the pictures given us by the old voyagers, and by Jourdan especially, of the island of Bermuda. You have all that can be brought from them in the pages of Malone and Chalmers; and you have the passage from *The Silver Watch Bell*, which seems to me more pertinent than anything they have produced. Do you find anything beyond what are the first elements in the conception of an island without inhabitant and in a stormy sea, except that both are in the popular language enchanted? Is there a single point in which we trace resemblance between ˙ the island of Prospero and Bermuda, which can be

regarded as peculiar and critical? Is there a single
expression in which we trace a verbal conformity
between the language of Shakespeare and the language of the voyagers? I ask in confidence; being
persuaded, as the result of no small attention to the
question, that nothing of the kind is to be found.
The remark, that the hogs of Bermuda suggested the
urchins which galled the feet of Caliban, may be
dismissed at once into the limbo of critical abortions.

I do not quote, because I think it useless, and you
have the words before you; but especially because I
can find no one clause or passage which seems peculiarly favourable to the inference which is drawn.
Indeed, in respect of the natural features, the critics
have scarcely attempted to trace out resemblance.
Their reliance is chiefly on what is metaphysical.
Both islands are under the influence of enchantment.
This is stated in very simple terms by the navigators
and by Jourdan. It is repeated by the continuator
of Stowe, not Stowe himself, who was dead, in a
passage which Mr. Douce, who quotes it, calls
" important;"* but in none of them have we more
on this subject, nor indeed quite so much as in the
passage which I have quoted from Tymme, who
gives what was no doubt the popular and received
belief.

Turn then to the quotation from *The Silver Watch
Bell*, to the passage in Stowe's continuator, or to the
slight notice in the accounts of the voyagers, and say
whether the enchantment of Bermuda can be regarded as having in any sense suggested the totally
dissimilar enchantment of the island of Prospero.

* *Illustrations of Shakespeare*, 8vo. 1807. vol. i. p. 6.

The utmost resemblance lies here, that in both cases
the storms are understood to be provoked by metaphysical agency. But it is metaphysical agency
belonging to two entirely distinct schools. The
enchantment of Bermuda is a branch of the mythology of the northern nations, a cold dark Scandi-
navian superstition, engendered in the imaginations
of men who acknowledged the power of wizards to
sell favourable winds, and whose evil spirit, by them
named Nicker, rode on the many waters. Has
Shakespeare any thing of this? Is there in this anything that could lead him to that philosophy, the
growth of another clime, the delusion of another
people, in which Prospero is a great adept, a philosophy which rests on the assumption that in stocks
and stones, and everything by which we are surrounded, fallen spirits dwell, who may be evoked by
those who know the *call*, and be made to execute
their commands? This philosophy originated in the
East, and the enchantment of the island of Shakespeare is accordingly clear and warm, and plainly of
Oriental tinting. It is also exhibited with much minuteness of detail. The aërial music, the unreal banquet, the richly varied visions, and the fires of Ariel
which gleam and burn not, have not a shadow of
resemblance to anything that is related of Bermuda.
Our canon forbids us to suppose that the one did or
could suggest the other.

I reserve the remarks which I have to make on the
supposed resemblance between the storm with which
the play opens, and the description of the storm in
which the two Englishmen were wrecked. For the
present I shall state generally, that there is the
same absence of particular points of resemblance in

respect of the storms as in respect of the islands;
and shall proceed at once to shew that there is
another island which has claims, that will not easily
be invalidated, to be the island which Shakespeare
had in view, and which he has made the scene of
the many beautiful and affecting incidents of this
delightful drama.   I shall shew that certain natural
features of this island are reflected in the drama,
and that there are traditions and superstitions connected with it, to which circumstances of *The
Tempest* bear some relation.   I must, however, do
the old critics the justice to say, that till this discovery (such I may call it) no island, as far as I
know, had a better claim to be regarded as the
island of Prospero than Bermuda.

I must also add, for on this point they appear to
have been misunderstood,† that no editor of Shakespeare has ever gone so far as to represent the island
of Bermuda as actually the scene of this play, but
only as having suggested the idea of a stormy,
deserted, and enchanted island, with a few (a very
few) of the subordinate circumstances.

---

† " Among the many claims which Bermuda has for a poetic
eye, we cannot for an instant forget that it is the scene of
Shakespeare's *Tempest*, and that here he conjured up the delicate
Ariel, who alone is worth the whole heaven of ancient mythology."
                    MOORE's *Epistle from the Bermudas.*
But it must be owned that Mr. Chalmers has given some encou-
ragement to this very prevalent mistake; for he speaks of Stephano as king of Bermuda, *Supplemental Apology*, p. 441 ; and
(*Apology*, p. 581) says, that the Poet " shewed great judgment
in causing, by enchantment, the king's ship to be wrecked on
' the still-vexed Bermoothes.' "

II.

LAMPEDUSA.

IF in a story, whether it be one of fact or fiction, we find the persons who are the actors in it carried to a deserted and enchanted island in a stormy sea, and we find such an island precisely in the situation, geographically, which the exigencies of the story require, can any supposition be more reasonable than that we have found the island which was in the mind of the writer, though the name of it may not occur in his work? If, in addition to its geographical position, we find that there are points of resemblance of a peculiar and critical nature, must not the probability be converted into certainty? Now, I mean to shew you that such an island there is.

The words of Ariel, on which so much stress has been laid by the advocates of the Bermudean theory,

> " in the deep nook, where once
> Thou call'dst me up at midnight to fetch dew
> From the still-vex'd Bermoothes,"

so far from serving as an index to the island which afforded what I may call the *prima stamina* of some part of this beautiful work, have proved, like the fires of the same spirit, a deluding light, which has led commentators and critics into seas far remote from those on which, with a story of Italy and Africa before them, their attention ought to have been directed. Their minds have been tossing on the Atlantic, when they ought to have been musing on the Mediterranean, " peering in maps for ports and piers and rocks," and, I add, diminutive and obscure islands which lie basking in the sun between Tunis and Naples. Where should Alonzo, when he returned from the marriage of Claribel, be wrecked, but on an island which lies between the port from which he sailed, and the port to which he was bound? Did we not know how much still remains to be done in the criticism of these plays, it would be scarcely credible that no one seems to have thought of tracing the line of Alonzo's track, or of speculating, with the map before him, on the island on which Prospero and Miranda may be supposed to have been cast. Yet such appears to be the case; for had the spirits of the commentators been attentive to those seas, and to the many islands with which they are studded, they could scarcely have failed to discover that there was *one* which has all needful points of resemblance to the island of Prospero, in the general, and withal others so peculiar and so minute, that there can, I think, be no hesitation in admitting that it is the island on which the incidents of the drama take place. The island I mean, is that known to geographers by the name LAMPEDUSA, or LAMPEDOSA, LIPADUSA, or LOPADUSA.

I call your attention, first, to its geographical position. It lies midway between Malta and the African coast. It is therefore precisely in the situation which the circumstances of every part of the story require. Sailors from Algiers land Sycorax on its shores. Prospero, sailing from an Italian port, and beating about at the mercy of the waves, is found at last with his lovely charge at Lampedusa. Alonzo, sailing from Tunis, and steering his course for Naples, is driven by a storm a little out of his track, and lights on Lampedusa.

In its dimensions, Lampedusa is what we may imagine Prospero's island to have been ; in circuit thirteen miles and a half.

Lampedusa is situated in a stormy sea. In the few notices which we find of it in the writers contemporary with Shakespeare, the name generally comes accompanied by the notice of a storm. In 1555, Andrew Doria anchored the fleet of Charles the Fifth on the island, after an engagement with the Turks : but a furious gale came on, when several of the ships were driven upon the rocks and lost. Crusius quotes from the narrative of a voyager, who in 1580, spent four days on the island, during the whole of which time there was one continued storm.

Lampedusa is in seas where the beautiful phenomenon is often seen, called by sailors the Querpo Santo, or the Fires of Saint Helmo. The commentators have told us that these fires are the fires of Ariel. But the very name of the island itself, *Lampedusa*, may seem to be derived, as Fazellus says it is, from *flames* such as Ariel's.

Lampedusa is a deserted island, and was so in the time of Shakespeare. The latest English traveller who has visited it, informs us that, " except a solitary anchoret or two, and a few occasional stragglers, it does not authentically appear to have been regularly inhabited in modern times." The Earl of Sandwich, who visited the island in 1739, found only one person living upon it. The old geographers, Crusius, Cluverius, and Sanuto, give the same account. But as from the general points of resemblance, we are now advancing to others which are critical and peculiar, I shall transcribe at large the best accounts I have been able to find of this little known and rarely visited island, and begin with Crusius :

" Anno 1580 in Quadragesima 4 triremibus Melita egressi sumus Africam (Barbariam vocant), prædæ causa petituri. Inter navigandum attigimus insulam Lampedosam, ab hominibus desertam, exiguo portu, vetusto et collapso castello ; parvum templum ibi in montis specu est, divisum bifariam. Altera ejus pars, S. Maria de Lampedosa vocatur : qui eo Christiani suis piraticis myoparonibus adveniunt, in ea offerunt nummos, vestes, panem, pulverem tormentarium, globos et alia, de quibus Turcæ nihil auferunt. Hujusmodi anathemata a Melitensibus triremibus Drepanum Siciliæ deferuntur, in Xenodocheium, nomine Annunciata, et magni æstimantur. Eodem modo in altera templi parte a Turcis oblationes fiunt. Aiunt qui non offerat, aut aliquid oblati auferat, nec restituit, non posse ab insula abire. Noctes ibi spectris tumultuosæ. Quarto die post, tempestatibus sedatis, inde Africam versus contendimus ; magnamque navim, oleo et dactylis onustam, cum Mauris amplius triginta, cepimus, et sic Melitem reversi sumus. Deinde mense Martio iterum Africam petentes, nullam prædam nacti sumus."—*Turco Græciæ, libri octo :* fol. Basil, 1584, p. 528.

The next is Fazellus :

" Nel mezo del mare tra Cercina e Sicilia, son l' isole Pelagie, e son tre, le quali son diserte ; cioè Lampedusa, Labenusa, e Scola, e son poco lontane l' una da l' altra. Lampedusa è la maggior di tutte, e gira intorno intorno dodici miglia, e ritiene l' antico nome, il quale gli fu posto per cagione de gli spessi baleni, e lampi, che vi si vedono, dove era già una fortezza del medesimo nome dell' Isola, e un castelletto, di cui si vedono ancor hoggi le reliquie. Vi è ancora una voragine, ò uno speco, et una chiesa dedicata alla Vergine Maria. Dalla parte di verso Ponente, è piena d' altissime, e di scoscese rupi, e di verso Leuante risguarda l' isola delle Gerbe, la quale si vede stare à guisa d' un' onda marina. Quest' isola e diventata famosa a' miei tempi, per cagion dell' armata di Carlo Quinto Imperadore, di cui era Capitano Antonio d' Oria Genovese, laquale miseramente vi fece naufragio. Perche l' anno M. D. L I. intorno a' quattro giorni di Luglio, essendosi partito da Messina il detto Antonio, insieme con quindeci Galere, con le quali egli portava vettovaglia alla città d' Africa, la quale l' Imperadore havea tolta di fresco a' Turchi,

levatasi in un subito una grandissima et inaspettata fortuna di
mare, venne a spinger l' armata di notte verso Lampedusa, e la gittò
da quella parte dell' Isola, ove gli scogli son più acuti, e si ruppero,
e vi morirono più di mille huomini, di diversi ordini, e conditioni ;
e se lo splendor d' un fulmine, e lo spesso fiammeggiar di baleni,
che venivano lucidissimi tra la grandissima pioggia non havessero
fatto vedere alle compagnie il miserando spettacolo dell' altre e per
questo avvertitele a ritornar con tutte le forze in dietro, tutta l' armata in quella spaventevol notte, andava in rovina."—*Dell His-
toria di Sicilia*, fol. 1628. p. 7.

Rather more particular is an anonymous French
writer of the seventeenth century :

" Cette isle mérite bien que j'en dise quelque chose ; puis que
nous en avons passé si prés.   Elle est à quatre-vingt milles de
Malthe, et à soixante d' Afrique, elle n' est habitée de personne,
mais elle est également frequentée des Turcs, il s'y voit une grotte
en maniere de chapelle, où sur la gauche en entrant est un autel
de nostre Dame, et à côté une maniere de representation mor-
tuaire de bois sur des treteaux, qu'on appelle tombeau de Maho-
met, avec un turban dessus, sur l' autel de la vierge est un
bassin, où la plus part de ceux de l'une et de l' autre religion,
qui abordent en cette isle, donnent quelque marque de leur devo-
tion, et quand ils n'y laissent point d'argent ils y laissent du pain,
du vin, de l' huile, et autres choses necessaires à la vie.   Monsieur
le grand prieur qui m' en contoit des particularités merveilleuses,
dit qu' on y trouve outre les choses necessaires à la vie comme
féves, vinaigre, huile, poisson marine ; il y a aussi des habits, des
trames, des planches, et enfin de tout ce que ce devot Chrestien, ou
Turc croit-y pouvoir estre utile à ceux qui abordent dans l' isle,
dont ils peuvent se servir librement, en cas qu'ils en ayent besoin
pour achever leur voyage, mais que qui que ce soit ne peut prendre
sans necessité que la punition suit de prés le crime, puisqu'on
ne peut sortir de l' isle jusqu'à ce qu'on ait fait restitution de
ce qu'on a pris n'y ayant que le seul pilotte reel des galères de
Malthe, qui ayt le pouvoir d'en enlever l' argent pour le porter à
nostre dame de Trapano en Sicile.   L' intention des uns et des
autres, quands ils y laissent des vivres, estant pour le secours de
quelques pauvres esclaves Chrestiens, ou Turcs, qui se sauvans
les uns de Barbarie et les autres de la Chrestienté dans de petites
barques, ou chaloupes portées par le vent en cette isle, y puissent
trouver de quoy subsister jusqu'à ce que quelque vaisseau de leur
religion venant à passer, les ramene en leur pays, ou le mauvais
tems, et peût-être la foiblesse de leurs petits bastimens ne leur a
pû permettre d' arriver.   Plusieurs qui mettoient en doute cette
merveille en ont reconnu euxmesme la verité par l' experience, et

sur tout les Corsaires Chrétiens, qui y ayans par plaisanterie dé-
robé quelques aspris ou tarins, ont fait quelque fois dix ou douze
fausses partances sans pouvoir gaigner la vent et le large, jusqu'à
ce qu'ils ayent restitué l' argent qu'ils avoient pris sur l'autel
sans necessité."—*Nouvelle Relation du Voyage et Description
exacte de l'Isle de Malthe*, &c. Paris, 12mo. 1679, p. 34—39.

I come to English voyagers; and first, the Earl
of Sandwich :

" It was not long, however, before we were relieved from all
our melancholy thoughts by a favourable gale of wind, which in
a few hours, brought us to an anchor in the road of Lampedosa,
distant about fifty miles from Kerkina. This island, according to
Pliny, was by the ancients called Lopedusa: it is about thirty
miles in circuit, produces a good deal of brush-wood, and has
several excellent springs of water, which were then more accep-
table to us than the most delicious wine. The whole of its inhabitants consists in one single hermit, who leads a solitary life in
an artificial grotto cut out of the rock, far from the intercourse of
mankind, whom he seems desirous to shun. His chief pleasure is
in the cultivation of a small garden and vineyard, which he main-
tains with great care and nicety. Joining to the cavern serving
for his habitation, is a chapel of the same nature, in which he
celebrates mass according to the Roman Catholic rite. Opposite
to this chapel is another grotto, in which is the tomb of a Turkish
saint, who died and was buried here at a time when the Grand
Signor's fleet was at anchor before the island. The hermit keeps
a lamp always burning at the head of this tomb, upon which account he remains unmolested by the Mahometans, who frequently
come to Lampedosa to water their ships and galleys. We were
assisted by this good old man to the utmost of his power, receiving
from him a calf and some other provisions, which entirely banished
the apprehensions we had of dying for hunger. The island of
Lampedosa was formerly inhabited by Christians, who were subject to the king of Naples and Sicily. Their city, now in ruins,
was situated at the extremity of a good port, on the eastern part
of the island. Notwithstanding they had erected for their defence
a pretty strong castle, they were always a very unhappy people,
being continually exposed to the depredations of the Turkish
cruisers; by whom, under the conduct of the renowned Barba-
rousse, they were in the end all made prisoners, and transported
to Algiers, ever since which the island has remained uninhabited."
—*Voyage round the Mediterranean*, 4to. 1799, p. 488.

But the best account is supplied by another countryman of our own, Captain W. H. Smyth, whose

account of the island contains many particulars not
found in the earlier writers, important in this enquiry, and whose testimony is the more valuable,
inasmuch as he had no Shakespearian theory in his
mind, and thought of nothing less than that he was
providing valuable matter for the illustration of our
greatest poet, when in the discharge of his official
duties he made the survey of the group of islands to
which Lampedusa belongs, which has been so highly
approved.

"LAMPEDUSA. At the distance of twenty-four miles south-west
by south, from Linosa, lies Lampedusa, a long narrow island
stretching east and west, and known to the ancients as Lopadusa.
It is thirteen miles and a half in circuit, with a level surface, but
abrupt craggy coasts, except to the south-east, where it shelves
from a height of nearly four hundred feet to a low shore, indented,
or rather serrated with many coves, of which the largest is called
the harbour, and deserves attention, as it was intended, at the
time Buonaparte disputed our demand of retaining Malta, that
this place, however unworthy, might be substituted for the valuable port of Valette.

"Lampedusa is a dependency of Sicily, and was given by
Alphonso to his valet Di Caro, with permission to build a tower
under baronial jurisdiction; but it was never inhabited on account,
it is gravely said, of the horrible spectres that haunted it. In
1667, it was acquired with the title of prince by the learned Ferdinand Tommasi of Palermo, a grandee of Spain, in whose family it
has ever since remained. There are vestiges of ancient habitations. In 1610, a barbarous inscription was found among the
ruins of Orlando's tower, now called the castle.

"A Sicilian legend states, that a vessel was wrecked on this
island, and that the only survivors were two Palermitan ladies,
Rosina and Clelia. They here found two hermits, Sinibald and
Guido, who, renouncing their ascetic life, married them; a population of course was the consequence, and the ruins near the castle
are adduced as vestiges of its respectability. But except a solitary
anchoret or two, and a few occasional stragglers, it does not
authentically appear to have been regularly inhabited in modern
times, until about ten or twelve years ago, when Mr. Fernandez,
an English gentleman, struck with its advantageous situation for
the establishment of a fishery, for rearing cattle, and refreshments
for Malta, and for opening a commercial intercourse with Barbary,

purchased a lease of it. The change of public affairs by the
general peace, with litigations, and several other causes unnecessary to relate here, have, however, ruined the speculation; and
when I last visited the island, I found the family of Mr. Fernandez, living in almost deserted solitude, in a house near the
great grotto, without the slightest protection from rovers, or, what
is worse, from infected vessels putting in there, which has ever
been a common practice. Twelve or fourteen Maltese peasants were
scattered about in the different caves near the cultivated parts.

" From the harbour, a stout wall, erected at the expense of Mr.
Fernandez, runs over in a north-west direction to the opposite
coast, entirely separating the broadest part of the eastern end,
which is under cultivation, from the rest of the island.   The
western parts are covered with dwarf olives, and a great variety
of plants, so that a good deal of firewood is cut and sent to Tri-
poli and Malta; and amongst this profusion there are plenty of
wild goats that used to annoy the farm considerably, until the
erection of the abovementioned wall: they still find a destructive
enemy, however, in the Numidian crane, called, from its graceful
gait, the damsel; these birds arrive in great numbers in May,
and delight to revel among the legumes, always planting a sen-
tinel to warn them of discovery during their ravages.

" From the south side, a bank extends several leagues, and
affords good anchorage under shelter of the island. On this bank
the celebrated Andrew Doria anchored the fleet of Charles the
Fifth, after having had an engagement with the Turks, that was
followed by a furious gale, in which some of the ships in coming
in, were driven against the cliffs between Cape Ponente and
Rabbit Island: those that, repairing to the east side of the island,
anchored in the Cala Piscina Bay, fared best.   Here too this in-
defatigable commander contrived to water the vessels, and repair
their damages.

" At a little distance from the Cala Croce, up a ravine in some
degree picturesque, is the residence of a celebrated recluse, and
the grotto is divided partly into a Catholic chapel and partly into
a Mahometan mosque.   This being at about twenty minutes' walk
from the harbour, the old gentleman had always sufficient time to
reconnoitre vessels that anchored, and according to the flag dis-
played, lighted up for the cross or the crescent, whence the pro-
verb of " the hermit of Lampedusa." The Turks, even when by
death or accident they found no inhabitant, always left a present
behind them, under the idea that without such a form they would
be unable to quit the place; but Coronelli should himself relate
this instance of superstition : ' Even writers worthy of confidence
assert that no one can reside in this island on account of the
phantasms, spectres, and horrible visions that appear in the night,
repose and quiet being banished by the formidable apparitions and

frightful dreams that fatally afflict with death-like terrors, whoever does remain there so much as one night. The Turks are
governed by a ridiculous superstitious idea, which is, that no one
would be able to go out of the island who did not leave something
there, or who had the hardihood to take away the merest trifle.
But the pure faith of the Knights of Malta is not so light and
vain, for they annually go thither with their galleys, and, collecting the offerings made to the forementioned church, take them over
to Malta, and there apply them to the support of the Hospital for
the Infirm.'

" I had observed such numbers of troglodytic caves, that I was
anxious to explore some of them, and when I was examining the
eastern bay of the harbour, I was just entering a small grotto,
when I was startled by seeing indented in deep characters the following warning:

Qui ritrovasi cadavere
Morto di peste in giugno, 1784."

*Memoir descriptive of the Resources of Sicily and its
Islands*, 4to. 1824, p. 285—288.

With this very valuable notice of the island, I close
my quotations. Indeed, the other notices which I
have collected from foreign geographers and travellers, do little more than present the same facts
which are already in evidence. I fear that the commentators and editors of Shakespeare are not the only
persons who are oftener found following in the track of
their predecessors, than giving us observations which
they have made in some new and unfrequented line
of research. The report of a Russian officer who was
employed by Prince Poniatowsky, to ascertain how
far this island would afford a convenient station for
ships, to be found in *The Naval Chronicle* for 1803,
yields nothing to our purpose. What is already
before us is, however, sufficient. You see that in the
time of Shakespeare, Lampedusa was not only a small
and desert island in a stormy sea, but that it also lay
under the reputation, or imputation shall I say, of

being enchanted; and I may add, that I have been told that *The Enchanted Island* is a familiar appellation by which Lampedusa is known among the mariners on the African coast.

The voyager in Crusius says, that the nights are disturbed by spectres. Cluverius: "The reason of its being abandoned is absurdly ascribed by some to the spectres and phantoms that haunt it; by others, to its unwholesome air, which causes frightful dreams and visions." Coronelli: "Even writers worthy of confidence assert that no one can remain on the island on account of phantasms, spectres, and horrible visions, that appear in the night, repose and quiet being banished by the formidable apparitions and frightful dreams that fatally afflict, with death-like terrors, whosoever does remain there so much as one night." Here is a sufficient basis for the enchantment under which the island of Prospero lay, and there is even a special resemblance between the spectres of the geographers, and the strange visions with which *The Tempest* abounds, the peopling of the air of the island with light unsubstantial Protean beings, who are employed sometimes to affright, but sometimes to comfort and encourage the hapless beings who are cast upon its shores. I do not say that the enchantment of *The Tempest* is throughout of the same character with the enchantment which popular belief attributed to Lampedusa, but only that there is a resemblance between them, and that we have now evidence before us that Lampedusa was regarded as being so enchanted. But there is one point in which the resemblance becomes so *special*, that it affords ground for the inference of *suggestion* in respect of the metaphysical agency of the drama. Persons visiting the island and acting unworthily there, were rendered incapable of leaving it, were spell-bound by a power that was superhuman, residing in one who was a lover of truth, and who punished deeds of fraud or rapine. Now compare with this one mode of the operations of Prospero :

> *Prospero.*   Say, my spirit,
> How fares the king and his followers ?
> *Ariel.*   Confin'd together
> In the same fashion as you gave in charge,
> Just as you left them, Sir ; all prisoners
> In the line-grove, which weather-fends your cell ;
> They cannot budge till your release . . . .
> *Prospero.* Though with their high wrongs I am struck
>   to the quick,
> Yet with my nobler reason 'gainst my fury
> Do I take part : the rarer action is
> In virtue than in vengeance : they being penitent,
> The sole drift of my purpose doth extend
> Not a frown further : Go, release them, Ariel.
>   *Act v. Sc. 1.*

Is there anything like this in the comparison of the enchantment of Bermuda, and the enchantment of the isle of Prospero ? but shall I a little overstep the line of strict decorum, and ask, my dear Sir, if your incredulity does not begin to give way ? whether it seems to you still possible that there should be an island of which such things were believed, so near the line of Alonzo's track, and yet that there should be no connection between its spells and its visions, and those which bound and beguiled Alonzo ? Place a mighty magician in the centre of those manifestations of superhuman power, which popular opinion attributed to Lampedusa, and you have the very body, form, and pressure of *The Tempest.*

This, at least, I claim to be allowed, that with these attributes of Lampedusa before us, there is no

occasion to go out into the Atlantic for any archetype
of the island of Prospero. What, I ask, is there in
the Bermudas which is not to be found also in Lampedusa? O yes, I beg pardon, the hogs, which Shakespeare has turned into urchins. Well, I give the commentators the hogs, and still contend that with no
more evidence before us than has already been
adduced, the claim of the Bermudas to have suggested the enchantment and other circumstances of
the play, is light as air, when compared with the
claim of this island of the Mediterranean. You will
allow me, for the present, to assume, what I shall
soon prove, that Shakespeare had the means of be-
coming acquainted with Lampedusa.

But I am not satisfied with the minor point of
comparative claim either with Bermuda or with any
other island. What I contend for, is the absolute
claim of Lampedusa to have been the island in the
Poet's mind when he drew the scenes of this drama,
and that circumstances connected with Lampedusa
suggested numerous circumstances in the play. I
pass on, therefore, to bring under your notice points
of resemblance between the geographical and real
island, and the island of the Poet, which seem to me
to be too peculiar and too critical to be accounted
for on any principle which shall exclude the Poet's
acquaintance, however it may have been acquired,
with the actual island.

The island of Prospero has a rocky coast. So
has Lampedusa. What can be inferred from this?
I willingly answer, Nothing ; absolutely nothing.
Monmouth is like Macedon. But then in these
rocks of Lampedusa there are hollows, such hollows
as we may imagine to have been human habitations

in the primeval ages. Captain Smyth calls them troglodytic caves, and found them actually inhabited. This is not common to every rock-bound island : and yet this peculiarity we find in the island of *The Tempest.* Caliban, like one of Mr. Fernandez's Maltese, inhabits one of these caverns :

" For I am all the subjects that you have,
Which first was mine own king : and *here you sty me*
In this hard rock, whiles you do keep from me
The rest of the island."   *Act* i. *Sc.* 2.

We have another allusion to these hollows in the conversation between the clowns concerning the wine : .

" *Trinculo.* O Stephano, hast any more of this ?
Stephano. The whole butt, man ; *my cellar is in a rock by the sea-side, where my wine is hid.*"   *Act* ii. *Sc.* 2.

Prospero, however, does not live the life of a troglodyte. He has his cell, a " full poor cell," yet capacious enough to contain himself and Miranda, with those volumes which he prized above his dukedom. It was the only place in the island that was fit for the habitation of human beings. Now just one such building there was at Lampedusa, the cell of the recluse, the Hermit of Lampedusa, where was the chapel and the mosque ready for any seaman of either faith. This cell is surely the origin of the cell of Prospero. I am told that there is an Italian engraving of it, but I have never seen it : and must be content with Captain Smyth's account of it. It stood " at a little distance from Cala Croce, up a ravine, in some degree picturesque." So is the cell of Prospero made picturesque by the line-grove with which it is shaded :

" In the line-grove which weather-fends your cell,"

the favourite retreat of Ariel.

The real cell has had solitary inhabitants, not wholly unlike Prospero : and you cannot have failed to observe how the tradition of which Captain Smyth speaks respecting the two Palermitan ladies, marks out Lampedusa as being a place which appeared to Italian imaginations a fit scene for such events as those which make up the story of *The Tempest*.

Again, there is a coincidence which would be very extraordinary if it were merely accidental, between the chief occupation of Caliban, and the labour imposed upon Ferdinand, on the one hand, and something which we find belonging to Lampedusa, on the other. Caliban's employment is collecting firewood. It may be but for the use of Prospero. But Ferdinand is employed in piling up thousands of logs of wood. This is not like the invention of a poet working at its own free pleasure. I should seek for an archetype, had I not already found one in the fact, that Malta is supplied with fire-wood from Lampedusa.

That the logs piled by Ferdinand were destined to this and no other use, is apparent from what Miranda says,

" When this burns,
'Twill weep for having wearied you :"
Act iii. *Sc.* 1.

in which she plainly alludes to the running of the sap when the logs were placed on the fire. They were logs of pine wood ; and this leads us to remark the consistency which runs through all the creations

of this exalted genius.   It was a cloven pine that
was the prison of Ariel.   Even the Algerine part of
the story of *The Tempest* has a kind of counterpart
in what little we know of the real history of Lampedusa, the ancient population of the island having
been carried away, as we have seen, by the Algerine,
Barbarossa.

I have not yet fully completed my proof; but
I would here pause to ask, whether there is not already sufficient to shew that the island of Lampedusa
is that on which the scenes of this drama are exhibited ; and whether you would think me presump-
tuous in requiring that in future editions of these
plays there should be in the accustomed place at the
foot of the Dramatis Personæ, the words

Scene—Lampedusa

This poor and barren island has of late been visited
only with a view to ascertain whether its port would
form a convenient station for Russian or British ships.
But English voyagers, as they pass from Malta to
the African coast, may hereafter call upon the master
to slacken his course as he passes within sight of an
island which is connected with the name and muse
of Shakespeare, while

" Pleas'd with the grateful scent old Ocean smiles."

For every thing which is touched by him seems to
be hallowed in the hearts of his countrymen.   You
must, I am sure, have observed the triumph of
Shakespeare, never perhaps more signally exhibited,
in the feelings of a living poet (long may he live!)
who, on first entering Italy, the land of song and art,

and ancient historical renown, turns from all these,
and rests on Shakespeare—

> " Am I in Italy ?   Is this the Mincius ?
> Are those the distant turrets of Verona ?
> And shall I sup where JULIET at the masque
> First saw and loved, and now by him who came
> That night a stranger, sleeps from age to age ? "
> ITALY.

I proceed to further evidence.*

III.

THE STORM—ARIOSTO.

I HAVE now to open another question connected
with the date, scene, and origin of this play. When
Shakespeare made the bold attempt at exhibiting
within his wooden O a storm at sea, had he any particular storm in view, or wrought he only with materials
such as every tempest and every case of shipwreck
would present to him?   I propose the question with
an intention of returning an answer : and the answer,
you will find, brings us again to Lampedusa.

The answer which is usually given, and the
answer which has hitherto been deemed incontrover-
tible, is that he had one particular storm in view,
and that the storm was that in which the Sea-Adven-
ture, having Sir George Somers and Sir Thomas

---

* I am bound to acknowledge, and I do so with great pleasure,
that I received many years ago the first suggestion of the identity
of the island of Prospero with Lampedusa, from one whose intimate acquaintance with books and their contents is well known to
all who have the pleasure of his acquaintance ; I mean Mr. Rodd,
the very ingenious, liberal, and respectable bookseller in Great
Newport-street.

Gates on board, was wrecked in the Bermudean seas. This is the point which Mr. Chalmers and Mr. Malone have taken so much pains to establish. Their position is (for it may be as well to repeat it) that the title of the play, and the circumstances of the storm in the first scene, were suggested by "the dreadful hurricane that dispersed the fleet of Sir George Somers and Sir Thomas Gates, in July 1609, on their passage with a large supply of provisions and men for the infant colony in Virginia; by which the Admiral ship, as it was called, having those commanders on board, was separated from the rest of the fleet, and wrecked on the island of Bermuda;" and that the account of that hurricane, which was published in the succeeding year, by Jourdan, in a pamphlet, entitled, *A Discovery of the Bermudas, otherwise called The Isle of Devils*, supplied Shakespeare with the particular incidents of the storm which he has delineated.*

I fear that I may be thought to have spoken already too freely of men to whom all critical readers of Shakespeare are so deeply indebted. I beg leave, therefore, to interpose an expression of my great respect for their labours, an expression which is most sincere; and of my desire that, for the unsubstantial criticism of which we have had so much during the last twenty years, we could return to the robust and serviceable criticism of the commentators of the last century. They may sometimes be mis-

---

* Jourdan's pamphlet may be found in Hackluyt, the modern quarto edition, vol. v. p. 555—558, for it is contained in four pages. There is a larger and better account of the storm and island by William Strachey, in Purchas; *Pilgrims*, Part iv. p. 1734—1741.

D

taken, as I deem them to be in much which they
have said on the play before us; but they abound in
remarks and illustrations of very great importance;
they set many things in a very just point of view, in
which not one reader in a thousand could, without
their aid, have placed them; and where, perhaps,
they do little to elucidate the author, they please,
by the variety and curiosity of the information which
they give us. It would be well, if we who follow
them, and profit so much by their labours, would
imitate the research and industry of some of them,
or could possess ourselves of the sagacity or genius
of others. But where I deem them mistaken, I
claim and shall exercise the right of saying so, without meaning offence to any: and I now ask any
one to look at the laboured argument of the two
commentators, and to compare the passages from
Jourdan's work, which they place in apposition with
passages in the first scene of this play, and then to
say whether there is anything beyond that similarity
which must always exist when the subject is a storm
at sea, and the wreck of a vessel on the rocky shore
of an island, whether the subject be treated in a
work of imagination, like *The Tempest*, or in such a
pedestrian narrative of real occurrences as that of
Jourdan. Mr. Malone has given the argument all
the advantage it could derive from the artful aid of
capitals and italics, but he seems to me to fail in
shewing coincidence in anything, except what has
been common to all storms and all disastrous ship-
wrecks from the beginning of the world. For a
critical or unusual circumstance, common to both,
we look in vain; nor is a verbal conformity, which
might betray that the Poet had recently read the

SHAKESPEARE'S TEMPEST. 35

narrative of Jourdan, anywhere to be found. No parallelism of numerous particulars, each of common occurrence. The parallelism on which much reliance is placed, of the safety, at last, of the Admiral, and the safety also of Alonzo, fails in this, that the escape of Alonzo was a necessary part of the story. I would deal fairly with commentators from whose labours I have received so much pleasure and instruction, and quote, if I saw anything that could be quoted with effect. But I find no such passage.

Besides, there is in the literature of the age of Shakespeare a description of *another storm* at sea, in which a vessel, having a king and prince on board, is wrecked, by a writer whose work was more likely to catch the attention of Shakespeare, and to fasten on his imagination, than Jourdan's. This description is by the pen of no less celebrated a poet than Ariosto, who of all the Italian poets was best known in England in the age of Elizabeth, and who had, of all the Italian poets, the greatest influence on our literature. The *Supposes* of Gascoign is a translation of the *Suppositi* of Ariosto. The structure of the Arcadia reminds of the abrupt transitions of the Orlando. The design of the Fairy Queen may be reasonably supposed to have been suggested by Ariosto, and the influence of the Italian over the English poet has been traced by Warton in many particulars. And, finally, Francis Harington translated the first fifty stanzas of the thirty-second book of the Orlando; and his elder brother, Sir John Harington, translated the rest of the poem before the year 1591, in which year the translation was published in a folio volume. Shall we then wonder if we find Shakespeare a reader of Ariosto, and indebted to him occasionally for an

incident or an expression? No writer was ever more
self-dependent than Shakespeare, but there is as certainly a pedigree of thoughts and expressions running
through the writings of the men of high poetic
renown, as there is of particular races in man. I
have mentioned the date of Harington's translation,
to shew that the Orlando might be read in English
in 1591, for the satisfaction of those who find a
pleasure in depreciating the learning and attainments of Shakespeare ; and, without entering far into
the question of the extent of Shakespeare's acquaintance with the ancient or modern languages, I willingly admit that Shakespeare read translations when
translations were provided for him. *The Tempest*
itself contains the most manifest evidence that he
read a translation of the Latin of Ovid, and of the
French of Montaigne. I shall shew you imme-

---

† This fallacy runs through the whole of Dr. Farmer's Essay :
*Shakespeare read translations, and therefore he could not read
the originals.* But who reads a Greek or Latin author as he
reads a newspaper? What writer for the public press (such
Shakespeare may be regarded) would read Plutarch in Greek, when
information from him was wanted for immediate use. It would,
methinks, be a very pedantic affair, were any one intending to
write a drama on a story told by Plutarch, to sit down, with the
Greek text before him, when he might find the whole matter in
English. Will the author of Ion do so, should he ever take a
story from Plutarch ? Again, the low appreciation of his classical
attainments taken by Dr. Farmer is so improbable, as to be absolutely ridiculous. Can any one seriously believe that he did not
know the meaning of such a word as *præclarissimus*, or that he
knew no more of Latin, than to put *hig, hag, hog*, in the mouth
of Sir Hugh. Dr. Farmer cannot have been serious. Mr. Hallam
has justly observed, that there are words which are derived from
the Latin which Shakespeare has used in what we may call their
etymological sense, shewing an acquaintance with the language
from whence their elements came. His offences against classical
propriety, in facts or quantity, are exceedingly few, and may
justly be regarded as mere oversights. But what was the attention

diately that it contains proof that he read this translation from the Italian of Ariosto. Whether he were necessitated to do so, or whether he did it from choice, is a question which it seems not to have entered into the mind of the Master of Emmanuel to think it necessary to ask. But the question of the learning is one of some extent and intricacy. I cannot enter into it in the text of this letter, but, for the honour of Shakespeare, I shall append a note containing a few hints on this subject, which those who follow Dr. Farmer may perhaps be induced to consider.†

---

to quantity in proper names in the English poets of that period? I could produce numerous instances of the neglect of it by professed scholars. What shall we think of Sir Arthur Gorges?

> " And on this floating bridge transport
> Old *Abydos* to Sestos' port."
> *Translation of Lucan*, fol. 1614. book ii. p. 77.

or of Thomas Farnaby, a schoolmaster, who joined with Milton in the Cambridge Verses on the death of Edward King?

" But though thy skill o'er *Lethe* and Styx have power."

I need not pursue this line of argument.

The grounds on which Dr. Farmer and others have rested their opinion of his want of acquaintance with the French and Italian languages are wholly insufficient. What reason is there to suppose that the scene of one of the plays, which is wholly in French, was not written by himself? But there is also a scene where the marks of his hand are quite evident, in which the dialogue alternates, French and English. Are we to suppose two persons concerned in the writing, as there are in the speaking? The argument upon the word *bras*, of which we have so much in Dr. Farmer, the commentators, and Mr. Douce's Illustrations, wholly fails. It is clear that Shakespeare meant the word to be pronounced as it is written; but then it is also clear that the English of his time preserved the sound of the final *s* long after it had been dropped by the French themselves. Thus, we keep still *embrace* and *vanbrace ;* and it is just as reasonable to infer, from Shakespeare's pun on this word, that he knew nothing of the true pronunciation of the French language, as it would be to infer

The storm described by Ariosto is the principal incident of the forty-first canto of the Orlando, and a magnificent and glorious passage it is. Shakespeare's obligations to it have never before been suggested. Of course, there must be in Ariosto, as there are also in Shakespeare, incidents and circumstances which are common to all storms. But what I contend for is this: that, beside those incidents and circumstances, there are some which are sufficiently critical and peculiar, to lead to the inference that there was *suggestion* on the part of the earlier poet, and *imitation* (a just and proper imitation) on the part of Shakespeare. Harington's translation is not a very common book, so that the whole passage may bear transcription:

> " A friendly gale at first their journey fitted,
> And bore them from the shore full far away;
> But afterward, within a little season,
> The wind discover'd his deceit and treason.

---

that Mrs. Piozzi knew nothing of French, because she has twisted a very ingenious string of rhymes with the word *Calais*, in pronouncing which, as also *Paris*, *Lyons*, *Dauphin*, and many other proper names, we have not yet thought proper to conform to the approved Parisian pronunciation. We may be wrong, and speak but after the school of Stratford-le-Bow; but an individual member of our nation is not to be censured as ignorant because he pronounces *bras* as the whole country pronounced it. There is a passage in Palsgrave, too long to be quoted in this note, respecting the pronunciation of the final *s* in French words, which is much to the purpose. In fact, it seems never to have occurred either to Dr. Farmer or Mr. Douce (both of whom, in reference to this word, have spoken very irreverently of Shakespeare), that there are *two* legitimate pronunciations extending to certain words in all languages, that of foreigners and that of natives. *Sans* we find in Shakespear's time written and printed *saunce;* and Anthony Munday, whose acquaintance with French will not be disputed, writes *souses*.

I shall in a future note say something on his knowledge of Italian.

9.

" First from the poop it changed to the side,
   Then to the prore at last it turned round ;
In one place long it never would abide,
   Which doth the pilot's wit and skill confound.
The surging waves swell still in higher pride,
   While Proteus' flock did more and more abound,
And seem to him as many deaths to threaten
As that ship's sides with divers waves are beaten.

10.

" Now in their face the wind, straight in their back,
   And forward this, and backward that it blows ;
Then on the side it makes the ship to crack :
   Among the mariners confusion grows :
The master ruin doubts, and present wrack,
   For none his will, nor none his meaning knows :
To whistle, beckon, cry, it nought avails,
Sometime to strike, sometime to turn their sails.

11.

" But none there was could hear, nor see, nor mark,
   Their ears so stopt, so dazzled were their eyes,
With weather so tempestuous and dark,
   And black thick clouds that with the storm did rise,
From whence sometimes great ghastly flames did spark,
   And thunder-claps that seem'd to rend the skies,
Which made them in a manner deaf and blind,
That no man understood the master's mind.

12.

" Nor less, nor much less fearful, is the sound
   The cruel tempest in the tackle makes ;
Yet each one for himself some business found,
   And to some special office him betakes :
One this untied, another that hath bound ;
He the main bowling now restrains, now slacks ;
Some take an oar, some at the pump take pain,
And pour the sea into the sea again.

13.

" Behold, a horrible and hideous blast
   That Boreas from his frozen lips doth send,
Doth backward force the sail against the mast,
   And makes the waves unto the skies ascend.
Then brake their oars, and rudder eke, at last,

Now nothing left from tempest to defend;
So that the ship was sway'd now quite aside,
And to the waves laid ope her naked side.

14.

" Then all aside the staggering ship did reel,
For one side quite beneath the water lay,
And on the t'other side the very keel
Above the water clear discern you may.
Then thought they all hope past, and down they kneel,
And unto God to take their souls did pray:
Worse danger grew than this when this was past,
By means the ship gan after leak so fast.

15.

" The wind, the waves, to them no respite gave,
But ready every hour to overthrow them :
Oft they were hoist so high upon the wave,
They thought the middle region was below them.
Ofttimes so low the same their vessel drave,
As though that Charon there his boat would shew them ;
Scant had they time and power to fetch their breath,
All things did threaten them so present death.

16.

" Thus all that night they could have no release;
But when the morning somewhat nearer drew,
And that by course the furious wind should cease
(A strange mishap), the wind then fiercer grew ;
And while their troubles more and more increase,
Behold a rock stood plainly in their view,
And right upon the same the spiteful blast
Bare them perforce, which made them all aghast.

17.

" Then did the master by all means essay
To steer out roomer, or to keep aloof,
Or, at the least, to strike sails if they may,
As in such danger was for their behoof.
But now the wind did bear so great a sway,
His enterprizes had but little proof ;
At last, with striving, yard and all was torn,
And part thereof into the sea was borne.

18.

" Then each man saw all hope of safety past,
No means there was the vessel to direct :
No help there was but all away are cast,
Wherefore their common safety they neglect ;

SHAKESPEARE'S TEMPEST. 41

But out they get the ship-boat, and in haste
Each man therein his life strives to protect:
Of king nor prince no man takes heed nor note,
But well was he could get him in the boat."

Had Shakespeare intended that his plays should
be perused in the closet, and not written them to be
exhibited in the theatres with much, in such a scene
as a storm scene, of what in technical language is
called *by-play*, he would, I think, have given us a
dialogue somewhat different from that which forms
the first scene of this play. Fletcher, in his *Sea
Voyage*, has shewn us how very pleasing words
may be set to the rough music of a storm. The
merit of Shakespeare, in this scene, is of a different
kind. He gives us the boisterousness of the seamen's
character. The sentences are brief and broken. A
want of sufficient acquaintance with the sea-terms
which he uses, and which does not seem to me to be
supplied by the nautical commentary which is found
in the last Variorum, occasions the scene to be somewhat obscure. But through the obscurity I seem to
perceive that kind of general resemblance to the
storm in Ariosto, which we may expect to find when
one poet has recently read the work of another,
when about to delineate such an event as that other
had described. But you will allow me to introduce
the scene itself, omitting only a very few immaterial
words :

Act i. Scene 1.

" *A tempestuous noise of thunder and lightning heard:
enter a ship-master and a boatswain.*

Master. Boatswain.
Boatswain. Here, master; what cheer ?
Master. Good: speak to the mariners; fall to't yarely, or we
run ourselves aground : bestir, bestir. [*Exit.*

Enter Mariners.

Boatswain. Heigh, my hearts: cheerly, cheerly, my hearts;
yare, yare ; take in the top-sail; tend to the master's whistle : blow
till thou burst thy wind, if room enough !

*Enter Alonzo, Sebastian, Anthonio, Ferdinand, Gonzalo,
and others.*

Alonzo. Good boatswain, have care : where is the master? play
the men.
Boatswain. I pray now, keep below.
Anthonio. Where is the master, boatswain?
Boatswain. Do you not hear him? you mar our labour:
keep your cabins : you do assist the storm.
Gonzalo. Nay, good, be patient.
Boatswain. When the sea is. Hence! what care these roarers
for the name of king? To cabin : silence : trouble us not.
Gonzalo. Good : yet remember whom thou hast aboard.
Boatswain. None that I more love than myself. You are a
counsellor: if you can command these elements to silence, and
work the peace of the present, we will not hand a rope more : use
your authority. If you cannot, give thanks you have lived so
long, and make yourself ready in your cabin for the mischance of
the hour, if it so hap. Cheerly, good hearts : out of our way, I say.
                                              [*Exit and re-enter.*
Boatswain. Down with the top-mast; yare, lower lower, bring
her to try with main course. A plague (*a cry within*) upon this
howling! They are louder than the weather, or our office . . . Yet
again? what do you here? shall we give o'er, and drown? have
you a mind to sink? . . Lay her a' hold.

Enter Mariners.

Mariners. All lost! to prayers, to prayers! all lost!
Boatswain. What, must our mouths be cold?
Gonzalo. The king and prince at prayers : let's assist them, for
our case is as their's . . . . (*a confused noise within*). Mercy on
us! we split, we split! Farewell, my wife, my children! Farewell, brother : we split, we split, we split!
Anthonio. Let's all sink with the king."

Now, besides whatever of general resemblance
there may be, these are the following minute and
critical circumstances common to both. We have
the master, and the master's whistle in both. I do
not say that to introduce the whistle might not occur

to both poets; but I think it improbable when both were seeking to fix the interest on a king and a prince in peril of drowning. We have the leaking of the ship in both; the striking of the sails in both; the falling to prayer in both; and, what is more remarkable, the contempt of rank and royalty in both. I do not say that all this may not be accidental, but I think it improbable that it should be so.

I ask you to think again on the stroke of nature, common to both poets, of the ascendency, in times of imminent peril and common distress, of the instinctive feelings over those which are superinduced and artificial :

" Of king nor prince no man takes heed nor note."

Shakespeare exhibits it though the bluntness and roughness of the seaman : " what care these roarers for the name of king? out of our way, I say." The sentiment suits the situation in both cases ; yet there are well attested instances of the maintenance of this respect in circumstances as hazardous and difficult as those into which either poet has brought his heroes.

But we have more respecting the circumstances of the storm than we find in the storm scene itself. Ariosto represents the passengers as being affrighted with " great ghastly flames" which appear to have been something more than mere common lightning. So we have Ariel in *The Tempest :*

" I boarded the king's ship : now on the beak,
Now in the waist, the deck, in every cabin,
I flam'd amazement : sometimes I'd divide,
And burn in many places ; on the top-mast,
The yards and bowsprit, would I flame distinctly,

Then meet and join: Jove's lightnings, the precursors
Of the dreadful thunder claps, more momentary
And sight-outrunning were not."   *Act* i. *Sc.* 2.

Verbal coincidences are perhaps few, but not, I think, slight. Shall I be accused of too great refinement if I point out three or four indications of connection, each lying in but a single word?

At the very opening of the second scene, where we find Miranda in discourse with her father, she says:

" If by your art, my dearest father, you have
Put the wild waters in this roar, *allay* them."

Compare with this what is said of the hermit, who meets Rogero on reaching the shore:

" And that he could, with one sign of the cross,
Allay the waves when they do highest toss."

There is, you will perceive, a threefold correspondency, the word, the person, and the action.

She proceeds:

" O, I have suffer'd
With those that I saw suffer! a brave vessel
Who had, no doubt, some noble creature in her,
Dash'd all to pieces. O, the *cry* did knock
Against my very heart! Poor souls! they perish'd."

The words of Ariosto were probably ringing in the Poet's ears:

" 'Twas lamentable then, to hear the *cries.*"

In Ariosto:

" The king of Affrick prais'd this offer kind,
And called it a good and *blessed* storm,
That caus'd him such a friend as this to find,
And thanks him for his offer."

Shakespeare was struck with this somewhat re-

markable use of the word *blessed*, and we seem to
owe to it, both Miranda's :

" Or *blessed* was't we did ?"

and Prospero's :

" But *blessedly* holp hither."

It may be said that there is nothing very critical
in the expression, " Water with berries in it," the
beverage which Prospero gave to Caliban.   To my
ear, however, the words do not sound like a free
creation of the Poet's own mind, and I cannot but
think that he was influenced by this line of Ariosto :

" But eating berries, drinking water clear,"

in which he describes the diet of the hermit who
welcomed Rogero.

But if I need your indulgence for these remarks, on
the value of which different estimates will be formed
by different persons, I shall need it still more for
another, in which any resemblance can be traced
only through the medium of a conjectural emendation.   You remember the passage in the storm scene,

" Blow, till thou burst thy wind, if room enough."

A meaning may undoubtedly be extracted from the
words, but it is poor for Shakespeare, and it has
gained little by the labour of the commentators.   Is
it not possible that this passage, as originally written
by Shakespeare, may have approached nearer than it
does at present, to a line in Ariosto ?

" To steer out roomer, or to keep aloof."

The precise meaning of the word *roomer*, I do not
profess to know, and I have consulted persons
acquainted with the language of sailors, in vain.

Possibly—it is a mere conjecture—the original editors
of this wholly posthumous play found the word as
unintelligible as it appears to us, and gave us the
present reading, still keeping near in sound to what
was written and spoken.*

---

* Respecting this word *roomer*, which I have not found in any
dictionary, Harington was conscious, when he used it, that he was
using a word which few would understand ; for he adds a marginal
note to the effect, that he speaks the language of mariners, and
will be understood only by them.   The only other place in which
I have found it, is in that very remarkable collection of sea-
terms made by Taylor, the sculler on the Thames, which has
a claim to insertion in a volume of notes on *The Tempest*, as he
says, " I think I have spoken heathen Greek, Utopian, or *Ber-
mudian*, to a great many readers in the description of this storm ;
but indeed I wrote it only for the understanding mariners' reading."   I quote the whole passage, though it is rather long, as
there are several sea-terms which occur in Shakespeare, and it is
in other respects a passage deserving attention :

" Midst darkness, lightning, thunder, sleet, and rain,
Remorseless winds and mercy-wanting main,
Amazement, horror, dread, from each man's face
Has chas'd away life's blood ; and in the place
Was sad despair, with hair heav'd up upright,
With ashy visage and with sad affright ;
As if grim death, with his all-murdering dart,
Had aiming been at each man's bloodless heart;
' Out,' cries the master, ' lower the top-sail, lower :'
Then up aloft runs scambling three or four;
But yet for all their hurly-burly haste,
Ere they got up, down tumbles sail and mast.
' Veer the main-sheet there,' then the master cried,
' Let rise the fore-tack on the larboard side :
Take in the fore-sail ; yare, good fellows, yare ;
Aluffe at helm there, ware no more, beware.
Steer south-south-east ; there, I say, ware, no more,
We are in danger of the leeward shore ;
Clear your main-brace, let go the bole in there,
Port, port the helm hard, romer come no near ;
Sound, sound, heave, heave the lead, what depth ? what depth ?'
' Fathom and a half, three all.'
Then with a whiff the winds again do puff,
And then the master cries ' Aluffe, aluffe ;

Let us next look to some of the incidents which occurred after the ship had gone to pieces, in which the king and prince had embarked. Rogero, the prince in Ariosto, betakes himself to the boat. The boat sinks, and he swims to shore. Ferdinand also, as you remember, saves himself from the wreck by swimming to the land. Compare Ariosto and Shakespeare :

21.

" Some swam awhile, some to the bottom sank,
   Some float upon the waves though being dead :
   Rogero, for the matter, never shrank,
   But still above the water keeps his head,
   And not far off he sees that rocky bank
   From which in vain he and his fellows fled.
   He thither laboureth to get with swimming,
   In hope to get upon the same by climbing.

22.

" With legs and arms he doth him so behave,
   That still he kept upon the floods aloft :

Make ready th' anchor, ready th' anchor, hoe,
Clear, clear the buoy-rope, steady, well steer'd, so ;
Hale up the boat, in sprit-sail there afore,
Blow wind, and burst, and then thou wilt give o'er.
Aluffe, clap helm a-lee, yea, yea ; done, done ;
Down down alow, into the hold, quick run ;
There's a plank sprung, something in hold did break :
Pump, bullies—carpenters, quick stop the leak ;
Once heave the lead again, and sound abaft ;
A shafnet less, seven all,
Let fall the anchor there, let fall ;
Man man the boat, a woat hale, up hale,
Top your main-yard, a port, veere, cable alow,
Ge way a-head, the boat there hoe, dee rowe ;
Well pumped, my hearts of gold, who says amends ?
East and by south, west and by north she wends :
This was a weather with a witness here,
But now we see the skies begin to clear :
To dinner hey, and let's at anchor ride,
Till winds grow gentler, and a smoother tide.' "
                The Praise of Hempseed—Works, fol. 1630,
                          p. 65, for 67, last series.

He blows out from his face the boist'rous wave,
That ready was to overwhelm him oft."

Thus Shakespeare :

" I saw him beat the surges under him,
And ride upon their backs ; he trod the water,
Whose enmity he flung aside, and breasted
The surge most swoln that met him : *his bold head
'Bove the contentious waves he kept,* and oar'd
Himself with his good arms in lusty stroke
To the shore, that o'er his wave-worn basis bow'd
As stooping to relieve him."   *Act* ii. *Sc.* 1.

This passage is laboured, and betrays marks of having been written with effort. In the words printed in the italic letter, I think I perceive that he recollected, at least, the passage in Ariosto. I could even persuade myself that he had the print of Rogero swimming to shore lying before him when he wrote this description of the swimming of Ferdinand. Rogero, at least, is there represented in the water, " keeping his head above the contentious waves, and oaring himself with his good arms in lusty stroke." Harington's Ariosto was the second book published in England, Broughton on the Revelation being the first, that was adorned with copper-plates.

The effect of calamity in rousing a slumbering conscience, another incident of human nature, is common to both poets. Thus Ariosto, still speaking of Rogero :

" But guilty conscience more doth him confound;
He now remembers he had plighted troth
To Bradamant, nor done as he had spoken ;
How to Renaldo he had made an oath,
And that the same by him was foully broken.
Most earnestly he now repents them both.
And calls to God for mercy."

And thus Shakespeare writing, as it seems to me, in emulation of this passage, represents Alonzo as having, in his misfortunes, called to mind his offence against Prospero :

> " Methought the billows spoke, and told me of it ;
> The winds did sing it to me ; and the thunder,
> That deep and dreadful organ-pipe, pronounced
> The name of Prosper; it did bass my trespass.
> Therefore my son i' the ooze is bedded ; and
> I'll seek him deeper than e'er plummet sounded,
> And with him there lie mudded."   *Act* iii. *Sc.* 3.

This, like the description of the swimming, has marks of effort and constraint. Had Shakespeare always written thus, he would have ranked but with the Marlowes, Kyds, and Peeles, of the age in which he lived.

The most remarkable circumstance remains to be mentioned. The storm described by Ariosto occurs in the same seas in which the voyagers in *The Tempest* are wrecked. The circumstances of this part of the story required two islands. Ariosto's geography is a little indistinct, or perhaps affected with the license given to a poet. The island with the steep cliffs which receives Rogero, is an island of the Mediterranean, inhabited only by a hermit. It seems not to be actually Lampedusa, but it has the attributes belonging to Lampedusa, which is the other island of this part of the poem, called by its softer name Lipadusa ;

> " Muta ivi legno, e verso l' Isoletta
> Di Lipadusa, fa ratto levarsi."   *Canto* xliii. *St.* 150.

which Harington adopts :

> " This Lipadusa is a little isle
> Distant from Africk shore some twenty mile."

E

and again :

"Near Lipadusa's steep and craggy cliffs."

Hofman, whom one rarely consults without find-ing something that is valuable, informs us that the Italian sailors call Lampedusa *La Casa d'Orlando*, in respect of its connection with this work of Ariosto.

We trace further resemblances between these two great poets. When Rogero reached the island,

"Upon the rock with much ado he crawl'd,
And sat upon the level ground in th' end :
When, lo, an aged man, whose head was bald,
And beard below his girdle did descend,
(That was a hermit that did there inhabit)
Come forth to him in godly reverent habit."

This is the hermit of Lampedusa, a kind of pro-totype of Prospero ; and, as we proceed, we are con-ducted to the hermit's cell, which we find like the cell of Prospero, sheltered by a grove of trees :

"The cell a chapel had on th' eastern side :
Upon the western side a grove or berie,
Forth of the which he did his food provide,
Small cheer, God wot, wherewith to make folks merry."

It was necessary to go thus into detail, because in no other way could the question be fully brought before you, whether Shakespeare, in delineating the storm and its attendant circumstances, prepared him-self by reading this canto of the Orlando. Not that I suppose he needed to repair to Ariosto, or to any other poet, to light up the fire in his own mind, but that *he chose to do so*, just as he chose to read translations when he might perhaps have read the originals.

Whether the evidence I have produced, each

portion of which I admit not to be very strong, but which, in the sum, I apprehend to be all-powerful, is sufficient to prove to you that Shakespeare was indebted (as far as he was indebted to any one) to Ariosto for the storm scene with which the play opens, and from which the play derives its name, you will admit that there is *much more* resemblance between the storm of Ariosto and the storm of Shakespeare, than there is between Shakespeare's storm and that which is described in the narrative of Jourdan; just as there is *much more* resemblance between Lampedusa and the isle of Prospero, than there is between that island and Bermuda.   There is therefore no longer any necessity for resorting to the narrative of the shipwreck of the two Englishmen for the origin of the storm in Shakespeare's play of *The Tempest*, any more than that we should look to the Bermudas for having suggested the enchantment, or any thing else, in the island of Prospero. Am I claiming too much from you, or any one, if I say that the Bermudean theory of the origin of this play is lost for ever?

"Now," to borrow an expression from that pleasant and patriotic old traveller, George Sandys, "shape we our course toward England," and enter into researches concerning this play, which will lie very much among the words and deeds of those eminent persons who adorned the period at which Shakespeare also lived. The Bermudean theory has hitherto been a cloud resting over this play, interrupting the view of some interesting circumstances belonging to it. In particular, it has kept out of sight what I believe to have been the true date of the composition of it, and one principal object, a patriotic one, which

Shakespeare had in view when he produced it. I
shall proceed in the investigation in the same fear-
less spirit in which I have pursued all my researches
into the Life or Writings of Shakespeare.

But before bidding adieu to the Bermudas, you
will perhaps enquire of me how the circumstances
of that island, which have appeared to other poets
susceptible of poetical adaptation, correspond with
any thing which we find in *The Tempest.* I have
already in part answered the question, by shewing
that to the poets contemporary with Shakespeare, Bermuda appeared, as it did to him, " still-vex'd," a solitary island in a tempestuous sea ; and I cannot find
that any of them have gone farther, and touched upon
any minuter peculiarity belonging to it. But the
case is different with the poets of the next genera-
tion. Bermuda has put off all its horrors, and appears a sunny, beautiful, rich, and fertile island,
with much to tempt people to make it their abode.
Who remembers not Waller's Battle of the Summer
Islands, with his description of Bermuda, with its
cedars, orange-trees, its pearl, coral, and ambergris?
But how few in comparison read Marvell, a man
who unfortunately, like Milton, gave himself up to
politics, when he might have been devoted an ac-
ceptable servant to the Muse. I will relieve the
dulness of this disquisition by giving his beautiful
lyric in full. It was written to sustain the spirits of
the puritan exiles, who, in the reign of Charles the
First, left their native shores to settle in Bermuda :

> " Where the remote Bermudas ride,
> In th' ocean's bosom unespy'd,
> From a small boat that row'd along,
> The listning winds received this song :

' What should we do but sing his praise,
That led us through the wat'ry maze,
Unto an isle so long unknown,
And yet far kinder than our own?
Where he the huge sea-monsters wracks,
That lift the deep upon their backs.
He lands us on a grassy stage,
Safe from the storms, and prelates' rage.
He gave us this eternal spring,
Which here enamels every thing:
And sends the fowls to us in care
On daily visits through the air.
He hangs in shades the orange bright,
Like golden lamps in a green night,
And does in the pomegranates close
Jewels more rich than Ormus shews.
He makes the figs our mouths to meet,
And throws the melons at our feet.
But apples, plants of such a price
No tree could ever bear them twice;
With cedars, chosen by his hand
From Lebanon, he stores the land.
And makes the hollow seas that roar,
Proclaim the ambergrace on shore.
He cast (of which we rather boast)
The Gospel's pearl upon our coast,
And in these rocks for us did frame
A temple where to sound his name.
Oh! let our voice his praise exalt,
Till it arrive at heaven's vault;
Which thence (perhaps) rebounding, may
Echo beyond the Mexique Bay.'
      Thus sung they in the English boat,
An holy and a chearful note;
·And all the way to guide the chime
With falling oars they kept the time."

You will observe how entirely dissimilar all the
colouring is from the colouring of the isle of Prospero. And if we come down to our own times, what
find we of resemblance in Moore's beautiful Epistle?
Verily with three such poems, Bermuda may well
relinquish its interest in *The Tempest.*

IV.

THE LINE-GROVE.—ARIEL'S SONG.—THE TEMPEST
AN EARLY PLAY.——THE CHRONOLOGICAL
ORDER.

YOU have perhaps smiled at the suggestion that
when Shakespeare wrote the lines in which he
describes Ferdinand saving himself by swimming,
he had before him the print which is prefixed to
the forty-first canto of Harington's Translation of
Ariosto. But I am inclined to think, that if our old
engravings were looked at with that view, it would
be found that they have influenced other poets besides Shakespeare.

What, indeed, is more usual with poets, when
they propose to describe any thing that is an object
of sight, than to place the object before them,
and, if the object be unattainable, some sensible representation of it? Perhaps, also, you may have
smiled at the suggestion that the common use of
words in themselves so little remarkable, as *allay*, or
cry, or *blessed*, may be taken as some evidence of
connection or suggestion; yet it is very certain, that
a later poet may sometimes be tracked in the footsteps of one who has gone before him, by the use of
a single word, the word itself not being remarkable.
Thus when in the Comus we read,

" Whilst from off the waters fleet,
Thus I set my *printless* feet,"

can we doubt that Milton remembered the passage
in this play,

> " And ye that on the sands with *printless* foot
> Do chace the ebbing Neptune, and do fly him
> When he comes back again :"   *Act* 5. *Sc.* 1.

or that when, in the exquisite Ode on the Nativity,
we find the line,

> " To hide her guilty front with *innocent* snow ;"

he remembered, and in one sense imitated, the line,

> " Cours'd one another down his *innocent* nose,"

of the *As You Like It*, his favourite play ?

So we are carried back by a single word, which
is to be sure one of less frequent occurrence, when
we read in the Lycidas, the most perfect of pastoral
elegies,

> " And hear the *unexpressive* nuptial song,
> In the blest kingdom meek of joy and love,"

to

> " The fair, the chaste, the *unexpressive* she,"

of the same play.   Milton, indeed, is for ever to be
tracked in the new fallen snow on his native land ;
and I cannot but think that some injustice is done
to Fletcher in referring, without quoting it, to the
beautiful little lyrical piece which is so palpably
imitated in some of the most admired parts of the
Penseroso.   Milton would occupy a considerable
space in the pedigree of poetic sentiment : but whatever he receives from his fathers he transmits with
the stamp of his own genius.

I have spoken of the *As You Like It*, as the
favourite play of Milton, and I think we may more

frequently trace him in that play than in any other.
I would not interpret such words in any over literal
spirit; but it seems as if Milton had this play more
particularly in his mind when, in the Allegro, he
speaks of Shakespeare thus :

> " Or. sweetest Shakespeare, fancy's child,
> Warble his native wood-notes wild ;"

or, when, in the *Theatrum* (the sentiment if not the
words must be his), he says, that " he pleaseth with
a certain wild and native elegance." The *As You
Like It*, was first given to the world in the same
book which contained *The Tempest* when first printed, the venerable folio of 1623, when Milton was
in his sixteenth year.

But we are wandering too far from our design.*

---

* Yet I will take advantage of the opportunity which the
modern system (unknown to the ancients) of writing with notes
appended, affords for introducing something more respecting Milton ; and first, I shall introduce to the reader a new piece of
evidence in the biography of the poet, which confirms what is said
on his having once seriously entertained the design of entering on
the study of the law ; and which seems also to shew something of
the kind of terms on which he lived with his father, a point, in his
biography, of some importance, as those who read Hacket's Life
of Williams know.   I have seen a copy of the *Natura Brevium*,
Tottel's Edition, 1584, on the fly-leaf of which is written, with
Milton's own hand :

> " Joñes Milton : me possidet.
> Det Christus studiis vela secunda meis."

The clear, beautiful and well-known autograph is not to be mistaken.   By another hand, is written on the same page :

> " Det Christus studiis vela secunda tuis."

I am not acquainted with the handwriting of the father, but
we can hardly be mistaken in ascribing this responsive sentiment
to him.

The elder Milton was not only devoted to music, but sometimes

I should now begin to introduce you to new
names, new scenes and new circumstances, while
endeavouring to establish what is my next position
concerning this play, namely, that, instead of being
the latest, as is generally supposed, it is one of the
earlier works of this great master. This enquiry
will have to be conducted on English ground; but
before quitting Lampedusa, I must invite you once
more to accompany me to the cell of Prospero, and to
the grove or berry of line trees by which it was
inclosed and protected from the weather. Shakespeare makes more of this line-grove than the editors,
commentators, and actors will allow us to perceive.
Indeed, if you look for the very word *line-grove*
in any verbal index to Shakespeare, you will not find
it; for the modern editors, in their discretion, have

---

attempted to embody his conceptions in verse. There is no occasion for the reserve of Mr. Todd, in attributing to him the Sonnet
to Lane; for it is evident that there was some kind of private
affection and regard between the Miltons and this very obscure
and indifferent poet, the " fine old Queen Elizabeth's gentleman"
of the *Theatrum Poetarum*. The disproportionate share of attention given to him in that work, might fairly lead to such an
inference; but the private regard seems to be put beyond doubt,
by the notice which is taken of the elder Milton in one of Lane's
unpublished poems, the *Triton's Trumpet*, of which there are
copies in the Museum and in the Public Library at Cambridge :

　" Those sweet, sweet parts *Meltonus* did compose."

The elder Milton was settled in Bread-street, where his son
was born, before the close of the reign of Elizabeth. I discovered
this fact embedded, like a fossil, in a huge mass of writing on
various subjects, where it might have remained for generations undiscovered, in the Common-Place Book of John Sanderson, a
Turkey merchant, a manuscript in the Lansdown department of
the British Museum. Sanderson was himself a writer of verse,
an encourager of the arts, and, in other points of view, a remarkable character. He has copied into this book a bond which was
executed on the fourth of March, in the forty-fifth year of Eliza-

chosen to alter the line in which it occurs, and we
now read,

" In the *lime*-grove which weather-fends your cell;"

an alteration this, you will say, of no great pith
and moment; but observe the effect of it. In the
first scene of the fourth act, when Prospero says to
Ariel, who comes in bringing the glittering apparel,
" Come, hang them on this line," he means on one
of the line-trees near his cell, which could hardly
have been mistaken, if the word of the original
copies, *line-grove*, had been allowed to keep its
place. But the ear having been long familiar to
lime-grove, the word suggested not the branches of
a tree so called, but a *cord-line*, and accordingly
when the play is represented, such a line is actually
drawn across the stage, and the glittering apparel is
hung upon it. Anything more remote from poetry
than this can scarcely be imagined.

There ensues some clumsy joking about the line,
among the clowns as they steal through the line-
grove with the murderous intent:

" *Stephano*. Mistress Line, is not this my jerkin? Now is
the jerkin under the line.
Trinculo. We steal by line and level, an't like your grace.

---

beth, in which " the new shop" is named of " John Milton,
scrivener, in Bread-street, London."

Dr. Farmer was greatly mistaken in the representation which
he gave of the sense of a well-known passage in the *Iconoclastes*.
But even when it is rightly understood, I cannot read it without
feeling that it is not quite just to Shakespeare; that it is too cold,
too dubious, too devoid of heart and affection, to have proceeded
from one who was once his worshipper, and who had owed so much
to him. Milton had, unfortunately, when he wrote that treatise,
given himself up to the world, and did not respect intellectual and
moral greatness as he respected it before.

Stephano. I thank thee for that jest; here's a garment for it: wit shall not go unrewarded, while I am king of this country. " Steal by line and level" is an excellent pass of pate.

The jests are worthless, suited to the clownish character of the clowns who utter them. This is, however, precisely one of those passages in which those who have closely observed the manner of Shakespeare, will be led to suspect that there is a meaning beside that which first meets the eye. At present I introduce them only to observe that they all refer to the line-trees, and not *(proh pudor!)* to a clothes' line.

The line-tree and the lime-tree are the same. The change has been made, because the latter is now the more usual appellation; but as late as the time of Elisha Cole, the other was the more familiar term : " line-tree, *tilia,* a tall tree, with broad leaves and fine flowers." The *linden* is a more refined appellation. Shakespeare was probably led to form the grove of this particular tree, by what he had observed of the use of it in the neighbourhood of London :

" The female line, says Gerard, or linden-tree, waxeth very great and thick, spreading forth her branches wide and far abroad, being a tree which yieldeth a most pleasant shadow, under and within whose boughs may be made brave summer-houses, and banquetting arbours; because the more it is surcharged with weight of timber, or such like, the better it doth flourish."

We may imagine in a grove of trees such as these, alcoves and bowers of delight in harmony with the young and lovely Miranda.

But, without attending to the particular kind of tree with which the cell of Prospero was surrounded, we can never perfectly understand the last of the

songs of Ariel, in which he exults in the prospect of
liberty :

" Where the bee sucks, there suck I."

Where does the bee suck, in preference to every
other flower, but in " the blossom that hangs on the
bough," the pendulous flowers of the line-tree ? You
have yourself told me, that when the line-trees at
Ham Green are in flower, whole hives of bees desert
the borders, and congregate upon them.   Ariel
meant to live in the line-grove :

> " Where the bee sucks, there suck I,
>   In a cowslip's bell I lie,
>   There I crouch when owls do cry,
>   On the bat's back I do fly
>   After summer merrily.
> Merrily, merrily, shall I live now
> Under the blossom that hangs on the bough."*

We have his life by day, and his life by night.
Whatever acceptance some other of my novelties
may find at your hands, I trust you will approve this

---

* This beautiful song has been unfortunate in other respects.
Few will approve of the way in which it is pointed by Mr. Malone,
whose principles of editorial duty did not allow enough either for
the freedom of ordinary dialogue, or the greater freedom which is
allowable in song-writing. If Shakespeare had been writing didac-
tically, it might have been proper to place a period at the word *crouch;*
but he was writing a song.   I have, therefore, disregarded the
punctuation of Mr. Malone, in the last Variorum edition, and
given it as it appears in the original copies, where it has all the
freedom which the Poet meant to allow himself.   When we hear
it sung to the music of Dr. Arne, the first line is altered thus :

" Where the bee sucks, there *lurk* I,"

to the manifest injury both of sense and melody.
Yet I can hardly bring myself to reject Theobald's amendment:

" On the bat's back I do fly
  After *sunset* merrily."

attempt to restore the line-grove to the consequence which Shakespeare meant to give it.   It seems to me that the use which is made of it, illustrates that infinite art of the Poet of which there are such numerous examples; shews the minuteness and exactness of his acquaintance with natural history; and adds a great beauty to the song of Ariel, which will no longer please only by the beautiful chime of the verse, but by its exact adaptation to the position of Ariel, and to what we may call the *ordonnance* of the whole drama.   The other songs of Ariel have the like relation to the story: but it has not, perhaps, been observed that the purpose of the song, so wild and beautiful,

" Full fathom five thy father lies,"

was to impress on the mind of Ferdinand the certainty that his father had been lost in the wreck, in order that he might feel himself at liberty to bestow himself, without a father's consent, on Miranda.   He alludes to this in the last act.

I cannot forbear to make, in this place, one or two remarks on editorial duties in general, and particularly on such duties as applied to Shakespeare.   We see the value of the old copies, and the wisdom of reading them, rather than the sophisticated text which the modern editors have given us, if we desire to know what Shakespeare really left to us.   They have, to be sure, some very strange corruptions; but then the very strangeness and the grossness work their own correction.   We see, at once, that Shakespeare did not write what is set down for him; and we can often see at once what he did write, through the strange disguise; while the modern editors, by the

application of their principles, or no-principles, too
frequently lay suspicion asleep, giving us a text
which, without being very bad, is not so good as that
which this fine spirit had itself bequeathed to us. It
is quite manifest, therefore, that in any modern edition the old copies (and here I cannot enter into the
question of the comparative value of the first and
second folio and of the quartos) should form the basis
of any new text, to the entire exclusion, in the first
instance, of the text of Rowe, and I am sorry to add,
of every other editor who has yet followed him. But
to this subject I shall recur towards the close of this
letter.

We see also the danger of tampering with the
text of a really great Poet, even in very minute particulars. It is but an *m* that has usurped upon an *n*
in a single passage, and yet what a disastrous effect
it has had on the conduct of the play. Let us hear
no more of the sarcasm of Young :

" While A.'s deposed, and B. with pomp restored."

It is now time that I should transport you into
those fresh fields and new pastures of which I spoke,
the fields of Elizabethan history, poetry and literature, which you have so successfully cultivated, while
I endeavour to ascertain the true period of the Poet's
life to which we are to refer this splendid production. I assume that we are no longer bound to
limit our enquiry to the period between 1610 and
1616, the year of the Poet's decease, but that we are
at liberty to fix the date of the play early or late in
his dramatic life, in the reign of Elizabeth or the
reign of James, according as the evidence shall at
last determine us. I need not remind you that this

play, like many others, remained long in manuscript before it was printed; that we have no entry of it on the Stationers' registry, nor any direct proof of its existence till we find it occupying the first place in the edition of the plays which was published by Heminge and Condell, his fellow-players, in 1623, seven years after the author's decease.

I have already announced to you what is my own impression, that this play is an early work; but I lay no stress on the circumstance, that when the plays were first collected into a volume, the first place was assigned to *The Tempest*. It is difficult to discover a principle on which the arrangement was made; and it is not difficult to divine other reasons beside priority of composition for the place assigned to it. Yet it may seem strange that if it were the last work, it should first meet the eye in such a collection. As little attention should I be inclined to give to what some persons have imagined they perceived in this play—intimations of its being a Poet's farewell, as if the retirement of Prospero were a kind of adumbration of the retirement of Shakespeare himself from the practice of the more innocent magic with which he had so long enchanted his countrymen.* Others

---

* This is so beautifully expressed by Mr. Campbell, that we might wish it to be true. "The Tempest has a sort of sacredness as the last work of the mighty workman. Shakespeare, as if conscious that it would be his last, and as if inspired to typify himself, has made its hero, a natural, a dignified and benevolent magician, who could conjure up spirits from the vasty deep, and command supernatural agency by the most seemingly natural and simple means. And this final play of our Poet has magic indeed; for what can be simpler in language than the courtship of Ferdinand and Miranda, and yet what can be more magical than the sympathy with which it subdues us? Here Shakespeare himself is Prospero, or rather the superior genius who commands both

have discerned in the style and sentiment marks of a period beyond the maturity of a Poet's life. But we see how extremely dubious and uncertain reasoning of this kind is, when we observe how often the most plausible conclusions of this kind have been dissipated by the discovery of some decisive evidence from without, fixing limits which no reasoning from the style or sentiments can justify any person in overleaping.

I suspect that all questions respecting the chronological order of these plays, must be decided by *testimony*, apart from any consideration of the general style and sentiments. The canon which Mr. Hallam has so well laid down,

" In criticism of all kinds, we must acquire a dogged habit of resisting testimony, when *res ipsa per se vociferatur* to the contrary," *

does not apply to these questions; for whose ears are so refined as to catch the voice which proclaims in each play the time of its composition ? " Spirits hear what spirits tell ;" but if I sought a proof of the want of clearness in the sound which these plays of themselves emit, or of aptitude to receive it, I should find it in the author of those words, who at different periods of his life caught sounds that

---

Prospero and Ariel. But the time was approaching when the potent sorcerer was to break his staff, and to bury it fathoms in the ocean—

" Deeper than did ever plummet sound."

That staff has never been, and never will be, recovered."

Remarks on the Life and Writings of William Shakspeare, prefixed to his Edition of the Plays, 8vo. 1838. p LXIII.

* *Introduction to the Literature of Europe*, &c. 8vo. 1839, vol. ii. p. 385.

were wholly dissimilar, and never caught the note
which was true.

Yet as this mode of determining the question has
been resorted to, I may venture to observe, though
on a point such as this I am bound to speak with
no small self-distrust, that I do not discern those
marks of long practice in the dramatic art, and of
the full maturity of a poet's genius, which some have
discovered in it. Of the general merit of its dramatic structure, I am fully sensible; of the skill with
which the characters are grouped, of the clearness
with which the story is developed, and the profusion with which some of the choicest flowers of poesy
are scattered every where in the reader's path. But
then I ask if this is not the case with *The Merchant
of Venice*, with *Romeo and Juliet*, with *A Midsummer Night's Dream*, all early plays; and with
As You Like It, and *Twelfth Night*, which, though
not so early as those which I have before mentioned,
were all upon the stage before the close of the reign
of Elizabeth? I ask where we are to look for evidence of greater maturity of moral taste, of dramatic
art, or poetic power in *The Tempest*, than may be
discovered in the plays I have just named? Perhaps *Romeo and Juliet* might be excepted, in which,
with all its beauties, and they are many, there are
decided marks of immaturity, something which reminds one of the taste which such a play as *The Jew
of Malta* was likely to create. Perhaps also in the
full maturity of his art he would not have so constructed his play as to render necessary the long
conversation in the second scene, which is evidently
intended for the information of the audience, and
not for carrying on the business of the drama: or

F

given us the two constrained passages which I have before quoted,* which seem to betray that they were written at a time when he was not fully aware of his power, and before he had found out the great secret that he wrote best when he committed himself fearlessly to his own transcendant genius. Perhaps also in the maturity of his powers he would not have copied, or at least not copied so servilely, the incantation of Medea, in Golding's Ovid, when he wrote the abjuration speech of Prospero, or the words of Montaigne, in his ideas of a new commonwealth. Perhaps also there is some want of dramatic skill in the abruptness of the charge against Ferdinand, that he had a sinister purpose in his appearance on the island. I may also remark, though it is a subject to which I never recur without pain, that *The Tempest,* in common with the other earlier plays, is disfigured by some of those impurities which are more rarely found in the late compositions.

On all this, however, I lay no great stress, and only introduce it as a *set-off* against remarks of the same kind which may have an opposite bearing. I go at once to the testimony, and in the first place ask you to look at the epilogue, and to tell me whether it is the work of one who had long been assured of the public favour, and who had won golden opinions from all sorts of men, or of the

---

* Dryden seems to have thought of one of those, as it appears to me, and he curtails it thus :

         " Sir, he may live,
   I saw him beat the billows under him
   And ride upon their backs ; I do not doubt
   He came alive to land."

diffident aspirant to dramatic fame. Mark the modest and timid address. It is Prospero who speaks :

> " Now my charms are all o'erthrown,
> And what strength I have's mine own ;
> Which is most faint : now, 'tis true,
> I must be here confin'd by you,
> Or sent to Naples. Let me not,
> Since I have my dukedom got,
> And pardon'd the deceiver, dwell
> In this bare island by your spell :
> But release me from my bands,
> With the help of your good hands.
> Gentle breath of yours my sails
> Must fill, or else my project fails,
> Which was to please. Now I want
> Spirits t' enforce, art to inchant ;
> And my ending is despair,
> Unless I be reliev'd by prayer ;
> Which pierces so that it assaults
> Mercy itself, and frees all faults.
> As you from crimes would pardon'd be,
> Let your indulgence set me free !"

To my ear these are not the words of one who was
taking his leave of the stage.

I would invite your attention, in the next place,
to what has not, I think, been observed before, that
a great change seems to have come over the mind of
Shakespeare soon after his fortieth year, respecting
the kind of stories which were best adapted to the
purposes of the drama, or on which he thought it
most befitting him to direct his own genius.

This is a subject of great interest and importance,
belonging immediately to the history of the Poet's
mind and studies. I shall therefore give in detail,
but in as concise a way as I am able, the proof that
such was the case.

Setting aside *The Tempest* for the present, the only
plays which, according to Mr. Malone and Mr. Chal-

mers, the two great critics in this department, were produced after the year 1606, were these :

TWELFTH NIGHT, assigned by Mr. Malone, to 1607, by Mr. Chalmers, to 1613.

A WINTER'S TALE, by Mr. Malone, to 1611, but by Mr. Chalmers, to 1601.

OTHELLO, by Mr. Malone, to 1604, by Mr. Chalmers, to 1614.

KING HENRY THE EIGHTH, by Mr. Malone, to 1603, by Mr. Chalmers, to 1613.

CYMBELINE, by Mr. Malone, to 1609, by Mr. Chalmers, to 1606.

TIMON, by Mr. Malone, to 1610, by Mr. Chalmers, to 1601.

JULIUS CÆSAR, by both, to 1607.

ANTHONY AND CLEOPATRA, by both, to 1608.

CORIOLANUS, by both, to 1609 or 1610.

Let no one hastily conclude, when they see such diverse dates assigned to these plays by the two critics of whom we are speaking, that there is no certainty to be obtained in respect of the dates of these compositions. Let them not advance to such a conclusion, when I add, that the chronology of both is, beyond all doubt, affected by very grievous mistakes. Mr. Malone is often in error, but the mistakes of Mr. Chalmers are most portentous.

Mr. Payne Collier, who has done so much for the illustration of the history of dramatic literature, has been the first to shew that *Othello*, so far from belonging to this late period, was a play in the reign of Elizabeth. The proof is complete, and none of the shadowy arguments of the older critics can possibly countervail it. In the household accounts of Sir Thomas Egerton, who was afterwards

Earl of Bridgewater, the following entry occurs under the date of the 6th of August, 1602, " To Burbidge's Players, for Othello, x *Li.*" *

Again, you may remember when, in 1828, I called your attention, at the British Museum, to the discovery which I had then made in the Diary of Manningham, † that *Twelfth Night* was performed in the year 1602, before the Benchers of the Middle Temple ; so that that play also belongs to the maiden reign, and not, according to Mr. Malone, to 1607, or to Mr. Chalmers, to 1613.

---

* *New Particulars regarding the Works of Shakspeare,* 12mo. 1836, p. 58.

† This Diary is the No. 5353 of the Harleian Manuscripts. It is quoted by Mr. Collier as " The Barrister's Diary ;" and in the same way it has been quoted by other persons since Mr. Collier shewed how much of curious information in our poetical antiquities it contains. I have not been satisfied without tracing to its author a manuscript which, beside other valuable notices of the persons and events of the time, contains two contemporary notices of Shakespeare. So many persons are mentioned who were friends and near relations of the writer of it, that this would have seemed to be an easy task. But I found it otherwise ; and it was not till I had recourse to the register of the Honourable Society of the Middle Temple, that I became convinced that the person whose writing the manuscript is, must be JOHN MANNING-HAM, a name not previously connected with literary history, who was entered of that society on March 16, 1597, and was called to the bar, June 7, 1605.

The period to which the manuscript relates, is from Christmas 1601, to April 14, 1608, when Manningham was living in London the life of an Inns of Court gentleman, mixing with poets, players, and lawyers, and sometimes with the divines and statesmen of the time. He was in the palace at Richmond at the very time when Queen Elizabeth died. The two notices of Shakespeare are of the performance of the *Twelfth Night,* in February, 1601-2 ; and a discreditable story which we find, taken I suppose from this manuscript originally, in the Life prefixed to Lamb's *Tales of Shakspeare.*

The book, though called a diary, is rather a book of memoranda. The larger portion of it consists of accounts of sermons

Cymbeline has no decisive marks of time, and the external evidence is scarcely worth regarding. It seems to me that it should be thrown back a year or two before the earlier of the two dates, and referred to the period when he produced *King Lear*. The plays arise out of the same history, and the passion of Cymbeline may seem to be a faint exhibition of the violence afterwards so fearfully represented in Lear. Shakespeare produced his plays in clusters.

King Henry the Eighth, I am prepared to prove (I use the strong term not without a corresponding conviction) to belong to the period immediately succeeding the death of Queen Elizabeth. It was Shakespeare's pious offering to the memory of a queen who had distinguished him by marks of her favour, and at the same time his gratulation to her successor, when, as Daniel says of the *Chorus Vatum* of the period, they all strove to bring the best offerings they were able to the time. Those who read the play attentively, and who are at the same time

---

which he heard at the Temple church, and other churches; but it is so full of *facetiæ* that we may regard it as

> " his table-book
> To write down what again he may repeat
> At some great table to deserve his meat."

He has preserved some curious and evidently authentic information, peculiar, it is believed, to this manuscript.

He who wrote this book must have written others like it. I wish the present notice may be the means of bringing to light any more of his remains. They would probably be found in the hands of the present representatives of Sir Richard Manningham, the physician, or of Manningham, the bishop of Chichester, both of whom were of his family. The relation who is so often mentioned in the diary, left him an estate at East Malling, in Kent, to which he retired about 1611. There is a long inscription in Latin, probably by John Manningham, on that relative's monument.

intimately acquainted with the state of public feeling, between the months of March and July in that
year, and the events which then occurred, will see
how curiously they are reflected in this play of
Shakespeare. It is indeed matter for surprise, that
it can ever have been thought that the gentle Shakespeare, who had a very quick perception of the deli-
cacies and proprieties of life, should have so far lost
sight of what was due to age and debility, to sex and
royalty, as to have presented on the public stage
a dying queen and the splendours of a coronation,
when an aged queen was on the throne, and evidently
passing, in a state of great depression and habitual
melancholy, to the grave.*

A *Winter's Tale* is placed, on very insufficient
evidence, by one critic in 1611, as appears by the

---

* The modern editors have gone so far as to place within crotchets the part of Cranmer's speech which relates to King James,
as if it were no part of the original design of this play. I have
not examined the editions, to ascertain who first took this liberty
with the page ; but in all later editions, critical or not critical,
the crotchets appear. And so accustomed has the eye become to
them, that they are supposed, even by critics on Shakespeare, to
have come down to us from the authentic copies of this play.
Mr. Armitage Brown, in his *Shakespeare's Autobiographical
Poems*, 8vo. 1838, p. 184, argues upon them as if they were
Shakespeare's own, or at least his original editor's. Mr. Brown
contends that the lines are not Shakespeare's, but I do not feel the
want of continuity of which he speaks, and to me they seem evidently to be from the same hand to which we are indebted for the
other portions of this eminently beautiful passage.

Dr. Johnson is one of those who refer *King Henry the Eighth*
to the reign of Elizabeth, in defiance of so many proprieties.
" These lines [those in crotchets] seem to have been inserted at
some revisal of the play, after the accession of King James."
Surely, much remains to be cut away, and much to be added,
before justice is done to this great author, or to those who
read him.

argument of the antagonist critic, who throws it back to 1601. In fact, it is a play remarkably destitute of notes of time; but there are some reasons for thinking that it was produced about the time when the *Twelfth Night* first appeared.

The Tempest is the play *de quo res agitur.*

And thus much I say, with the lively Dr. Farmer, for the far-famed essays on the chronological order.

Let us now see what plays remain for the later period of the Poet's life. They are only *Julius Cæsar, Anthony and Cleopatra, Coriolanus, Timon;* and to these I will add *Troilus and Cressida,* as possibly of this era. So that it is now evident, that as Shakespeare grew older, his muse grew severer; that he forsook the lighter subjects in which, at the beginning of his career, he delighted, and devoted himself to what Sir William Alexander calls "Monarchic Tragedies," stories of Rome and Greece and Troy. If we look a little above them in the list, we shall find that the two next plays in the chronological arrangement, are *Macbeth* and *King Lear,* which are of the same grave character, and exhibit the high passions and deep sorrows of the great.

Is it probable then that *The Tempest,* a work in every respect so unlike to these, should have been produced contemporaneously with them? That when he was engaged on themes such as these, he should for once have deviated into the paths of romance, in which in the early years of his life, he had delighted to wander; that he should have mixed with them one comedy, and one comedy only. I am still on probabilities only. Shew me probabilities equally cogent on the other part.

Now, take a view of the dramas which he produced in the earlier period of his dramatic career,
while still Elizabeth, whom he had the good for-
tune to please, was on the throne. We will set
aside the English histories, and with them the
Merry Wives may go. Little attention need be
paid to *The Taming of the Shrew, The Comedy
of Errors*, and *The Two Gentlemen of Verona*, as
being works of uncertain, though early date, of
inferior power, and, perhaps, not wholly his. View
him then in the vigour of his morning genius. The
plays are, *Love Labours Lost, A Midsummer Night's
Dream, Romeo and Juliet, The Merchant of Venice,
All's Well that Ends Well, Much Ado about Nothing,
As You Like It, Twelfth Night, A Winter's Tale,
Hamlet* and *Othello*. It is evident that *The Tempest*
classes with many of these plays. It classes with
them as a romantic drama. It classes with them as
a tale of France or Italy. It classes with several
of them in its style and sentiments. I ask for
the countervailing probabilities in favour of a later
date.

I pass in the following section to something which
approaches to the character of direct and positive
testimony. My witnesses are persons well known
to you, Francis Meres, Ben Jonson, and Sir Walter
Raleigh.

V.

MERES—BEN JONSON—RALEIGH—FLORIO—
THE DEAD INDIAN.

I DO not mean that we have evidence which does not require some degree of working out from the persons I have mentioned, to the existence of *The Tempest* at an early period of Shakespeare's dramatic life. If that had been the case, most assuredly you would not have been troubled with the probabilities leading to this conclusion. But I cannot but think that the evidence, especially that of Meres and Jonson, when it is once fairly brought before you, will do as much to produce conviction as that more direct evidence which has removed the *Twelfth Night* back into the reign of Elizabeth.

You are well acquainted with the importance of Meres' testimony in the question of the chronological order. He gives the names of twelve plays of Shakespeare, in existence when he published his work, the date of which upon the title-page is 1598. With such a testimony, and with so many dates in the books of the worshipful Company of Stationers, and so many printed copies of single plays with dates on the title-pages, no one can have a right to say that there is nothing certain in these enquiries? Meres' list of the twelve plays has hitherto been regarded as unfavourable to the opinion that *The Tempest* is an early play. I mean to shew that it is strong in favour of that opinion.

SHAKESPEARE'S TEMPEST.   75

The title of his work is *Palladis Tamia, Wit's Treasury, being the Second Part of Wit's Commonwealth.* It is a book of similes, and belongs to a series of publications intended for the especial use of young scholars, in the composition of themes. *England's Parnassus,* and the *Belvedere,* works of great importance in our poetical antiquities, belong to this series.* One chapter of the *Palladis Tamia* is intitled, *A Comparative Discourse of our English Poets with the Greek, Latin, and Italian Poets.* This chapter contains several notices of Shakespeare, of which the following is the most remarkable:

" As Plautus and Seneca are accounted the best for comedy and tragedy among the Latins, so Shakespear among the English is the most excellent in both kinds for the stage ; for comedy, witness his *Gentlemen of Verona,* his *Errors,* his *Love Labours*

---

* Meres' volume has been often referred to of late, but no one has shewn its peculiar nature. The first in the series to which it belongs, is intitled, *Politeuphuia, Wit's Commonwealth.* This consists of " A Methodical Collection of the most Choice and Select *Admonitions and Sentences.*" The collector was Robert Allott. Meres' book of *Similes* was the next. Then came a book of *Examples,* under the title of *Wit's Theatre of the Little World.* This appears to have been Allott's. The fourth was *England's Parnassus,* consisting of passages from the *Poets,* common-placed. This also was Allott's. A similar work was printed in the same year, 1600, which may seem as if it were to be referred to the same design, intitled, *Belvedere, or the Garden of the Muses,* containing similar excerpts, but rarely extending beyond two lines, as being the fitter on that account for the use of students tasked to the production of themes. We may add that *England's Helicon,* which is a collection of pastoral and lyrical pieces, was first published in the same year. Allott, Meres, and Bodenham, were the persons chiefly concerned in the production of all these works.

Dr. Farmer, and Warton, and, following them, Sir Egerton Brydges, and others, have intimated that this Robert Allott is the person of that name who was the publisher of the second folio. But this might easily be shewn to be a mistake.

Lost, his *Love Labours Won,* his *Midsummer Night's Dream,*
and his *Merchant of Venice :* for tragedy, his *Richard the
Second, Richard the Third, Henry the Fourth, King John,
Titus Andronicus,* and his *Romeo and Juliet,*" p. 282.

The question is, does Meres in this list recognize the existence of *The Tempest* in 1598, or does
he not?

It is manifest that *The Tempest* is not in his list
eo nomine; but what play, I ask, did he intend by
Love Labours Won?

Those who answer out of book will say at once,
All's Well that Ends Well. You, who have been
accustomed to think on all subjects connected with
Shakespeare for yourself, will pause before you
return this answer.

A passing remark of Dr. Farmer, in the Essay on
the Learning, first identified the *All's Well* with the
Love Labours Won. The remark has since been
caught up and repeated by a thousand voices.

Yet it was made in the most casual, random, and
hasty manner imaginable. It was supported by
no kind of argument or evidence; and I cannot find
that any persons who have repeated it after him,
have shewn any probable grounds for the opinion.

The leading features of the story in *All's Well,*
cannot be said to be aptly represented by the title
in Meres' list.

But this is trifling. If ever there was a play
which itself bespoke its own title from the beginning,
it is this :

> " We must away,
> Our waggon is prepar'd, and time revives us :
> *All's Well that Ends Well ;* still the fine's the crown,
> Whate'er the course the end is the renown."
>
> *Act* iv. *Sc.* 4.

Again :

> " *All's Well that Ends Well*, yet,
> Though time seem so adverse and means unfit."
>
> *Act* v. *Sc.* 1.

And as if this were not sufficient, in the epilogue :

> " The King's a beggar now the play is done ;
> *All is well ended* if this suit is won."

And so much, I say again, with Dr. Farmer himself, for the claim of this play.

But if not to the *All's Well*, to what play of Shakespeare was this title once attached ? I answer, that of the existing plays, there is only *The Tempest*, to which it can be supposed to belong: and so long as it suits so well with what is a main incident of this piece, we shall not be driven to the gratuitous and improbable supposition that a play once so called is lost.

> " *Enter* FERDINAND, *bearing a log :*
>
> *Ferdinand.*—There be some sports are painful, and their labour
> Delight in them sets off ; some kinds of baseness
> Are nobly undergone ; and most poor matters
> Point to rich ends. This my mean task
> Would be as heavy to me as odious, but
> The mistress which I serve, quickens what's dead,
> And makes my labours pleasures :   O, she is
> Ten times more gentle than her father's crabbed ;
> And he's composed of harshness.   I must remove
> Some thousands of these logs, and pile them up,
> Upon a sore injunction : my sweet mistress
> Weeps when she sees me work ; and says, such baseness
> Had never like executor.   I forget :
> But these sweet thoughts do even refresh my labours."
>
> *Act* iii. *Sc.* 1.

Again :

> " for your sake
> Am I this patient log-man."

And Prospero afterwards tells him :

> " All thy vexations
> Were but my trials of thy love; and thou
> Hast strangely stood the test."   *Act* iv. *Sc.* 1.

Here then, are the *Love Labours.* In the end they *won* the lady

> " So perfect and so peerless."

If you resist this evidence, I may enquire, what other play in your opinion was meant ?

I suspect that the play had originally a double title, *The Tempest, or Love Labours Won ;* just as another of the plays had a double title, *Twelfth Night, or What you Will.** Meres may seem to

---

* The inaptitude of this title has been matter of surprise to the critics : but the second part of it shews very plainly that the Poet was quite as sensible as any of his commentators have been, how little it had to do with the subject of the play : and indeed, if I am right as to the origin of the name, it was given on a very peculiar kind of suggestion.

Manningham, when he tells us that *Twelfth Night* was per- formed in the Middle Temple Hall, indulges in some conjectures respecting the origin of the plot. He sees in it some resemblance to the *Menœchmi* of Plautus, but he tells us that it resembles more nearly an Italian play called the *Inganni.* Now there are more Italian plays than one called *Gl' Inganni* earlier than the time of Shakespeare. To one of these Shakespeare appears to have owed some obligations. But in the search for the *Ingannis*, I met with a play called the *Ingannati ;* and it was soon evident that it was on this play, and not on any of the *Ingannis*, that Shakes- peare founded the serious part of his *Twelfth Night.* I say founded, meaning only that he took from it the plot, and a few of the minor incidents ; for the language and all the magnificent poetry of *Twelfth Night,* is all his own. Every thing respecting Malvolio (except the name, which is the Malevolti of the Italian dramatist) is wholly his, and supplies the place of another under- plot in the Italian. The *Ingannati* was one of the plays of the *Academici Intronati* of Sienna, and a passage in Ginguéné, (vol. vi. p. 303) which has been pointed out to me, shews that it attained a popularity in many parts of Europe, and was translated into the French language. The play has this peculiarity, that it has a long induction, and besides this a very long prologue. Now

have chosen to call it by the second title, for the sake of the opposition to the title of the play which he had named immediately before it, the *Love Labours Lost*.

On the whole, then, I submit that we have Meres' testimony to the existence of *The Tempest* as a play of Shakespeare, in 1598.

It would add some strength to this conviction could any remarkable correspondencies be shewn between

---

in the prologue the following passage is found, and I leave it to the reader to judge whether, in the absence of a better reason, it is not probable that the words which I have printed in italics, caught the eye of Shakespeare, when he was deliberating on the name to be given to his play, and determined him to the somewhat inapt choice which he has made :—" La favola ; e nuova non piu per altri tempi vista ne letta ne meno altronde cavata che della loro industriosa zucca, onde si cavorno ancho *la notte di Beffana* le sorti vostre, per le qua li vi parve, che gl' Intronati vi mordesser tanto in su quel fatto del dichiarare, e diceste, che gli havevan cosi mala lingua."

The Italian drama is at present an unexplored mine of matter for Shakespeare illustration.

May I add, as a supplement to a former note, that the use which Shakespeare made of the *Ingannati* seems to afford evidence that he read the Italian language. French and other translations there may have been of this play, but none, it is believed, into English. Observe also, how, in *Othello*, he Italianates in the use of the word *unhoused* :

" But that I love the gentle Desdemona,
I would not my *unhoused* free condition
Put into circumscription and confine
For the sea's worth."   *Act* i. *Sc.* 2.

Unhoused to an English ear suggests nothing which a man would not willingly resign. But it would be different with an Italian.

I will just add to this already superabundant note, that Malvolio is intended to be a personation of the puritan of the time, the worst parts of the character being, however, selected for the purpose of making it odious and contemptible : and that the exorcistical scene is a ridicule of an actual occurrence of the time, wherein Shakespeare appears as usual on the side of sense and truth.

The Tempest and the *Love Labours Lost*, a title to which the other title was evidently meant to be respondent. That *Love Labours Lost* is an earlier play is manifest from its abounding so much in rhymes, which is the case with those other plays which were wholly or partly his, produced indisputably when first he became a writer for the stage. But there is one remarkable correspondency which seems to point to such a connection between these two plays as we should expect to exist between two with corresponding titles, and it is this; that the stories of these two plays (and it is the case with them alone of all the romantic dramas) have a certain relation to events and characters of real history, so that we are able to fix a chronological period near to which the time of the action must be referred. In connection with this, there is the further correspondency, that of all the romantic dramas of Shakespeare, *The Tempest* and *Love Labours Lost*, are the only two for which no origins of the stories have yet been discovered. I venture to predict, that when the origins are found, they will be found in one and the same volume; some very rare book of romances or dramas in the literature of France, Navarre, Spain, or Italy.

On the indisputable allusion to a work of a remarkable person of the time, John Florio, in *The Tempest*, and the supposed allusion to the same person in the *Love Labours Lost*, I shall speak, when I come to consider the difficulties which press against the supposition of so early a date for *The Tempest*, as I have assigned to it.

To settle the chronology of the plays of Jonson, is a less difficult task than to perform the same

service for Shakespeare. There is no room to question that *Every Man in his Humour*, was his first
play; and the notice of it in Henslow's book, in
November, 1596, shews that it was then in existence.* This play is introduced by a prologue, in
which, as it seems to me, there is much matter bearing on the present enquiry. Mr. Gifford, indeed,
contends that there is no sufficient evidence that
Jonson alluded to Shakespeare, in the satiric strokes
with which that prologue abounds. I, on the contrary part, am ready to maintain, that it is quite
incredible that there should be so many strokes by
which Shakespeare is hit, and yet that not one of
them should be intended to fall upon him: and that
it is also incredible, that there should be in that
prologue so many strokes which admit of being
interpreted as blows aimed at *The Tempest* in particular, and yet that none of them were intended
for it.

Especially, as it is evident that Jonson began his
dramatic career with the intention of reforming the
English stage, and bringing the English drama
nearer to the models of antiquity. Jonson set up in his
own mind Plautus as the writer to be followed in
comedy, and Seneca, in tragedy. He was, therefore,
by his principles bound to seek to banish from the
stage the kind of plays with which Shakespeare was
at that period delighting the public, the histories
and the romantic dramas, and to endeavour to sub-
stitute for them comedies, in which the humours of

---

* *Works of Ben Jonson*, Gifford's edition, 8vo. 1816, vol. i.
p. xxv. of the Memoirs.

G

men were exhibited as men then were, or stately tragedies, with no mixture of what is comic.

Nor, whatever may be thought of the bearing of this prologue, can it be denied that Jonson does pointedly, in another place, direct his satire against this very play of *The Tempest :* " Such as beget Tales, Tempests, and such like drolleries."

And especially, moreover, as Jonson did not at any time forbear to speak what were his opinions concerning his contemporaries, and especially Shakespeare. Jonson was a somewhat rough and impracticable person, to which is to be attributed that his passage through life was so difficult and rugged ; a remarkable contrast to the smooth and pleasant course which the facile and kindly temper of Shakespeare secured for him. But I entirely acquit him of any jealousy, envy, or other bad passion, towards his illustrious contemporary, and, in one sense, rival, and I had almost said towards any other of his contemporaries on whom he has pronounced unfavourable judgments. He was too great a man for the mean passions of jealousy or envy. What he wrote, or what he said in his Conversation with Drummond, who deserves, in my opinion, our thanks for having carefully preserved it, which appears to be disparaging, were but critical judgments, and each of them would, I think, be found to be just, would any one bring them to the test.

With Shakespeare, in particular, my persuasion is, that he lived on terms of the most perfect amity : that their intercourse was frequent, and that there was a reciprocal respect, attachment, nay affection. I most heartily believe that Jonson did really " love the man and honour his memory, on this side idolatry, as much as any;" and that the noble tribute which he poured out to the memory of his friend, which some have strangely regarded as a reluctant and deficient testimony, is not a mere artificial poem written for the nonce, but the effusion of a mind deeply imbued with admiration and love.

But is this the nature of those relations in which men of letters stand to each other—that what each one does must be approved by all the others if they wish to be regarded, now and hereafter, as his friends?

Shakespeare and Jonson had different views of the dramatic art, and each wrote according to his own views. Shakespeare, perhaps, as little approved some things in Jonson, as Jonson did the violations of dramatic proprieties, the introduction on the stage of beings not *in rerum naturâ*, and the occasional unfiled expressions of Shakespeare; only his judgments have not descended to us.

Besides, the flouts and girds which one dramatist is found casting out against another, may often be referred to the intention of keeping up the spirit of the theatre, or may be likened to the sarcasms heard at the bar passing between persons who, when they have left the court, are the best friends imaginable. When Jonson wrote the prologue, which has led to these observations, his play was to be produced at the theatre called the Rose, while *The Tempest*, and the rest of Shakespeare's plays, were exhibited by his own company at the Globe, and the theatre in the Black Friars. The language of the prologue may easily be interpreted thus, in perfect consistency with that good feeling which, I believe, to have ever existed between them : " Our rivals at the other house are attempting impossibilities, or are degrading the stage by the introduction of masques and monsters. We mean to shew you, in the production of a new poet, what comedy ought to be, and what we design to make it."

This, in addition to the sober judgment of Jonson, who was doubless sincere in his preference of the classical to the romantic drama; for that, after all, was the question between them.

But I must no longer withhold from you the prologue itself, and the remarks which I have to make upon it:

" Though need make many poets, and some such
As art and nature have not bettered much,
Yet ours for want hath not so loved the stage,
As he dare serve the ill customs of the age,
Or purchase your delight at such a rate,
As, for it, he himself must justly hate:
To make a child now swaddled, to proceed
Man, and then shoot up, in one beard and weed,
Past threescore years; or, with three rusty swords,
And help of some few foot-and-half-foot words,
Fight over York and Lancaster's long jars,
And in the tyring-house bring wounds to scars.
He rather prays you will be pleased to see
One such to-day, as other plays should be;
Where neither chorus wafts you o'er the seas,
Nor creaking throne comes down the boys to please:
Nor nimble squib is seen to make afeard
The gentlewomen; nor rolled bullet heard,
To say, it thunders: nor tempestuous drum
Rumbles, to tell you when the storm doth come.
But deeds and language, such as men do use,
And persons, such as comedy would choose,
When she would shew an image of the times,
And sport with human follies, not with crimes.
Except we make them such, by loving still
Our popular errors, when we know they 're ill.
I mean such errors as you'll all confess,
By laughing at them, they deserve no less:
Which when you heartily do, there's hope left then,
You, that have so graced monsters, may like men."

Neglect of the unities, the introduction of beings

not human, the attempt at representations for which
the theatres were inadequate, are the general points of
attack. The special points are these : (1) The same
play exhibiting a character in infancy and age :
(2) The wars of York and Lancaster : (3) The removing the scene to a distant country by means of
a chorus : (4) The descent of a creaking throne :
(5) Thunder and lightning : (6) Monsters. Now,
within the scope of these objections, Shakespeare ob-
viously stands ; and the utmost that can be said by
those who would defend Jonson from the charge of
having here made an attack upon Shakespeare is this,
that not he alone was within the scope of these objections, but that other dramatists stood so with him.
But when of the special points of attack we find the
three last in *The Tempest,* it can hardly, I think, be
reasonably doubted, that that particular play was in
the view of Jonson when he wrote the prologue.
The " Monster," must be Caliban, " graced" as he
has always been by the favour of the multitude,
nor graced unworthily. The " creaking throne," is
the throne of Juno, as she descends in the Masque ;
the " nimble squib," is the lightning during the storm,
with which the play opens ; and the " tempestuous
drum," is the thunder which accompanied the lightning. But observe, I beg you, the word *tempestuous :*

" nor *tempestuous* drum
Rumbles, to tell you when the storm doth come :"

corresponding to the stage direction for the first
scene of this play, as originally printed : " A *tempestuous* noise of thunder and lightning heard."

I say, as originally printed, for the modern editors
have altered it, and given us a diluted phraseology ;
" a storm, with thunder and lightning." We should

look in vain also, in some of the modern editions, the last Variorum for instance, for the descent of Juno. I had referred, in some notes on this prologue, made long ago, from the line,

" Nor creaking throne comes down the boys to please,"

to this descent of Juno : and was perplexed when, attempting to verify it, I turned to Malone, and found that there was no distinct proof that Juno did descend. In fact, Malone has left out the stage direction of the original copies, " Juno descends," which is placed in those copies in apposition with the words of Iris :

" The queen o' the sky,
Whose watery arch and messenger am I,
Bids thee leave these, and with her sovereign grace,
Here on this grass-plot, in this very place,
To come and sport : her peacocks fly amain,
Approach, rich Ceres, her to entertain." *Act* iv. *Sc.* 1.

So that it is clear she came from above, her car or throne drawn by peacocks ; a proof that the mechanism of the English theatre in the time of Elizabeth, had reached no small degree of perfection.

I could even imagine that there is a severer stroke at Shakespeare in the play itself, as it was originally written ; for I need not inform you that there are two very different editions of *Every Man in his Humour*. I allude to the " old worn rags," in the long speech of Lorenzo, on the true nature of poetry, which exhibits Jonson in a very favourable point of view, a passage which was omitted when the comedy was revised. Can he allude to Shakespeare, of whom inferior dramatists complained that he was " beautified with their feathers," and who, in this play, uses the very words of Golding and Florio ?

The commentators tell us, that it was Jonson who taught Shakespeare the true pronunciation of the name Stephano, which is always right in *The Tempest*, but wrong in *The Merchant of Venice*. How they know this is not in evidence ; but is it not possible that Shakespeare yielded himself to Jonson in a more material point, and that the change to which we have adverted, as having come over him about the year 1604, may be attributed in some measure to Jonson's influence ? Have we gained any thing by this ? Shakespeare is great in whatever he undertook ; but it is to the earlier works of Shakespeare, as to the earlier works of Milton, that we turn for our sweetest pleasures.

It has occurred to me, and I throw out the remark for your consideration, and that of the public, that Shakespeare seems to have accepted the kind of challenge which is made in this prologue. True it is that he had written the romantic drama, that he had disregarded the unities, and brought upon the stage goddesses and earth-born monsters ; but it did not therefore follow that he was insensible to the beauty and propriety of the classical drama, or saw not that the peculiar humours of living men were a proper subject for the stage : and he produces *The Merry Wives of Windsor*, a regular comedy, which is remarkable for the variety of humours of men which it presents, and for being the fullest exhibition which Shakespeare has given us of the domestic life and manners of his countrymen. What comedy of Jonson's can be compared with this ?

To return to the point which was to be proved. Jonson's prologue being written in 1596, is a proof of the existence of *The Tempest* in that year.

And to the spring or summer of 1596, I am disposed, on a full consideration of the whole evidence,
to assign it.

You, who have been accustomed to look upon
these plays with an eye at the same time to the subjects which, at the time of their first appearance,
occupied the public attention, and who know how
frequently Shakespeare is found alluding to what
we may call the topics of the day, will now ask yourself what, in the spring and summer of that year,
especially engaged the attention of the people of
England? I also will ask the question, because out
of the answer which must be given to that question,
I propose to draw another proof that the play belongs
to the period to which I have assigned it. Now I answer, without the slightest fear of contradiction, that
the event which, in the early months of that year, would
be the theme of wonder, the subject of the conversation of the whole people of London, was the return of
Sir Walter Raleigh and his companions from the expedition to Guiana, and the very extraordinary reports
which they made of what they had seen and heard.
The expedition was performed in the year 1595; and
early in 1596 appeared the pamphlet of Raleigh, in
which he gave an account of what they had done,
seen, and heard; a pamphlet which would excite
wonder indeed, and would tempt cupidity, but which
could not, I will venture to say, but make his judicious friends grieve. The very title is enough to
condemn it, boastful and ridiculous: " The Discovery of the large, rich, and beautiful Empire of
Guiana, with a Relation of the great and golden city
of Manoa (which the Spaniards call El Dorado), and
the provinces of Emeria, Arromaia, Amapaia, and
other countries, with their Rivers adjoining. Per-

formed in the year 1595, by Sir Walter Raleigh, knight, Captain of Her Majesty's Guard, Lord Warden of the Stannaries, and Her Highness' Lieutenant-General of the county of Cornwall."

Such is the title which ushers us to a book stuffed with the most improbable reports, quite sufficient to bring the author within the class of travellers satirized in this play, who " mistake the truth," and deal in " vouched rarities" which are " beyond credit."

I shall soon shew that there are special points in which this pamphlet of Raleigh's is attacked ; but were there no such specialties, I should regard the general truth that there is so much ridicule in this play of travellers' wonders, of foreign plantations, new schemes of government, and the like, as no mean proof that it appeared at no great distance of time after this pamphlet, because there was no other book of travels which, in the time of Shakespeare, excited so much the public attention as this, or which was so open to ridicule, and yet, in some points of view, so dangerously misleading. We do little justice to Shakespeare if we regard him only as one who ministered to the public entertainment on the stage and in the closet. He ever looked, I believe, to the best welfare of his countrymen, and exerted himself to promote it, by correcting popular delusions, and diffusing just sentiments among them ;*

---

* For this, the English nation, I may rather say, the human race, have incurred " a debt immense, of endless gratitude." His plays are full of moral wisdom of the most exalted and purest kind, often wrapped up in expressions so beautiful that every one loves to remember them, and so terse that they are easily remembered, and often, I have no doubt, determine many in every age to a particular course of action, humane and Christian. But I rather allude to what we may call the vices of the day. Shakespeare mixed with society of every kind. He was the intimate friend of the Earls of Southampton and Pembroke : he was one of the

and a book which held out the tempting prospect of unbounded wealth, which seemed to require only that a hand should be stretched out to grasp it, was a dangerous experiment on popular credulity, which it was worthy such a master-hand as Shakespeare's to seek to counteract.

Raleigh, too, was no favourite with Shakespeare, or rather with the political party to which Shakespeare belonged. Shakespeare was of the Essex faction, to which his patron, the Earl of Southampton, was, for himself so unfortunately, attached. Shakespeare's

---

society of wits and poets, who resorted to the Mermaid : and he mixed with the common-place people who formed the burgery of Stratford. He had in his character something of all; but he was superior to the prejudices of any one class, and he felt his call to be to witness against what was evil in every class. I allude particularly to the ineffable ridicule which he throws on the practice of duelling in the *Twelfth Night*; to the rebuke of drunkenness in *Othello*; to the scorn of popish and puritan miracles in *King Lear* and the *Twelfth Night*. He also bears a noble testimony against the severe treatment of heretics, a vice of the age :

> " It is an heretic that makes the fire,
> Not she that burns in it."
> A WINTER'S TALE, *Act* ii. *Sc.* 3.

and, without unreasonably extending this note, he goes far before his age, and bears his testimony against the use of the rack to extort confessions :

> " Aye, but I fear you speak upon the rack :
> *Where men enforced do speak any thing.*"
> THE MERCHANT OF VENICE, *Act* iii. *Sc.* 1.

and he takes care, in what follows, that the audience should associate the words with the idea of treason. See the honest boldness of this lover of truth and of man ! He had all the politicians of the time, mean and dishonest men ! against him. The cries of their victims might be ringing in the dark chambers of the Tower whose turrets were in sight, when he and his fellows were repeating this sentiment at the Globe. I hope it was received with a plaudite.

company represented the deposition of King Richard
the Second, on the day before the insurrection, at
the special request of Sir Gilly Meyrick. Shakespeare has a beautiful compliment to Essex, in his
King Henry the Fifth, and a biting gird at Cecil,
and possibly also at Mountjoy, in the *Much Ado*.
Is it then surprising that he should not omit such
an opportunity of attacking Raleigh ? But he does
it fairly and honourably, in the manner of a dramatist,
it is true, but not exaggerating Raleigh's faults and
follies. He does not insinuate dishonesty of purpose. His satire is confined to the gross improba-
bility of his statements : and, looking again at the
pamphlet, which I happen to possess in the original
edition, I see no reason to charge Raleigh, as Hume
has done, with having circulated these delusive accounts with a fraudful intention ; but neither can I
at all agree with Mr. Fraser Tytler, in the estimate
which he has taken of this tract. Raleigh seems to
me to fall justly within the scope of Shakespeare's
censure. I cannot find that he makes the distinction
of which Mr. Tytler speaks, between the things he
saw and the things he heard, but has given to the
things which he only heard, the full weight of his
own personal authority, or at least circulates them
with the credit of his own full belief. Camden, the
learned, the wise, the candid, and the just, whose
fine character I can never contemplate but with the
highest delight, has spoken of this tract in a manner
which becomes his high reputation, and hints at the
true source of the mistakes, " the sanguine complec-
tion of Raleigh's own hopes and desires." As *The
Tempest* did not appear till after the publication of
Raleigh's pamphlet, Shakespeare is not to be re*

garded as one of those of whom Raleigh, in his dedication to the Lord Admiral, so bitterly complains.

But I have not yet given you the special proof that this tract of Raleigh's is the subject of Shakespeare's ridicule in this play. Turn then to a speech of Gonzalo, in the third scene of the third act, in which these lines occur:

> " or that there were such men
> Whose heads stood in their breasts? which now we find
> Each putter out on five for one* will bring us
> Good warrant of."

Now, compare Raleigh:

" Next unto Arui, there are two rivers, Atoica and Caora, and on that branch which is called Caora, are a nation of people *whose heads appear not above their shoulders*, which though it may be thought a mere fable, yet for mine own part, I am resolved it is true, because every child in the provinces of Arromaia and Canuri affirm the same: they are called Ewaipanoma: *they are reported to have their eyes in their shoulders, and their mouths in the middle of their breasts.*" P. 70.

There is more about them. He asserts, in another part of his book, his entire belief in the story: and in his enumeration of the several nations at p. 91, he writes seriously, thus:

" To the west of Caroli, are divers nations of canibals, and of those Ewaipanoma *without heads.*"

The reader will judge whether the improbable parts of his narrative were not his own. Where was his anatomy? Where his philosophy?

---

* This is the old text, except that I have changed *of* into *on.* In Malone, it is " of one for five." The subject has been well illustrated by the commentators. Persons going on long voyages sometimes deposited sums of money with persons at home, to receive three, four, or five times the amount on their return, according to the distance and supposed danger of the expedition. A copy of an insurance of this kind may be seen in the MS. of Sanderson, to which I have referred in a former note.

Shakespeare alludes again to the " men whose
heads do grow beneath their shoulders" in *Othello* ;
and he returns to the attack upon Raleigh's discreditable pamphlet, in *The Merry Wives of Windsor*,
which immediately succeeded *The Tempest*, or at
least appeared very soon after it : " She is a region
of Guiana, all gold and bounty."

Thus, to shew Shakespeare bearing an effective
testimony against public and mischievous delusions
such as these (let the spirit of Raleigh pardon me
for this one reflection) at the time when the testimony was most wanted, will be regarded as some
proof of the utility of an enquiry into the time when
the several plays were composed.   A true chronology
of the plays will prevent also a world of mistake in
the annotation.   Thus, Shakespeare, contrary to all
probability, considering how little his party esteemed
Raleigh, is represented as having intended to rebuke
Coke for his rude behaviour to Raleigh on his trial,
in the allusion to *thou-ing* in the *Twelfth Night*.   It
was the conjecture of one of the commentators, and
such hold has it gained on the public mind, that Mr.
Tytler has transferred it to his entertaining Life of
Raleigh, p. 266.   I have already shewn that *Twelfth
Night* was written two or three years before the
trial took place.

Am I then presuming beyond what the evidence
justifies, in referring *The Tempest*, not, with Mr.
Malone, to 1611, or Mr. Chalmers, to 1613, but to
the summer of 1596, when the excitement produced
by Raleigh's publication was at its height ?

But before I can expect that you or my other
readers will acquiesce in this violent dislocation, I

must endeavour to remove one difficulty which I find pressing against the argument:—I mean the palpable reference to a passage in Florio's translation of Montaigne, which translation was not published in print, as far as our bibliographical knowledge at present extends, before 1603. I shall, then, attend to Mr. Chalmers' argument on the " dead Indian," which will be more easily disposed of.

In the first scene of the second act, the following lines are given to Gonzalo, the honest old courtier who had befriended Prospero in his distress, who is, however, somewhat given to prosing, an anticipation of Polonius :

" I' the commonwealth I would by contraries
Execute all things ; for no kind of traffic
Would I admit; no name of magistrate ;
Letters should not be known ; riches, poverty,
And use of service, none ; contract, succession,
Bourn, bound of land, tilth, vineyard, none :
No use of metal, corn, or wine, or oil :
No occupation; all men idle, all,
And women too; but innocent and pure ;
No sovereignty :
All things in common nature should produce,
Without sweat or endeavour : treason, felony,
Sword, pike, knife, gun, or need of any engine,
Would I not have ; but nature should bring forth,
Of its own kind, all foison, all abundance,
To feed my innocent people."

Any person acquainted with the manner of Shakespeare would perceive that a passage such as this must have an *origin* out of the mind of the Poet himself; and it is one of the many services which Shakespeare criticism owes to the almost forgotten Capell, that he was the first to detect the origin in Montaigne, in whose Essays, as translated by Florio, we find the following passage :

" It is a nation, would I answer Plato, that hath no kind of
traffic, no knowledge of letters, no intelligence of numbers, no
name of magistrate nor of politic superiority; no use of service, of
riches, or of poverty; no contracts, no successions, no dividences,
no occupation, but idle; no respect of kindred, but common; no
apparel, but natural; no manuring of lands; no use of wine,
corn, or metal. The very words that import lying, falsehood,
treason, dissimulation, covetousness, envy, detraction, and pardon,
are never heard of amongst them."—Book i. ch. 30.

That Shakespeare had read this passage of Montaigne is most evident, and also that he had read
it in this particular translation which Florio had
made. An additional interest has been given to the
circumstance by the recent discovery of a copy of
Florio's translation with the name of Shakespeare
in it as the possessor, written by the Poet's own
hand.*

---

* This book was bought for the British Museum for the sum
of one hundred and twenty pounds, being, without the autograph,
worth about fifteen shillings. At a previous auction it had brought
one hundred guineas. Such is the reverence with which Englishmen regard every thing that is nearly connected with Shakespeare.

An account of this volume is given in the *Archæologia*, vol.
xxvii. p. 113—123, by Sir Frederick Madden. I willingly add
my testimony, whatever it may be worth, to the genuineness of
the Poet's autograph. But will my friend, Sir Frederick Madden,
excuse me, if I express my dissent from his proposal, that the
name of *Shakespeare* shall be transformed into the shape in which
it appears in that autograph, *Shakspere?* In coming to that conclusion, Sir Frederick Madden seems to have overlooked two
important points. First, that the practice in writing of the individual is not the proper guide to what should be the present
orthography. If it were, we must no longer write Lady Jane
Grey, a fac-simile of whose autograph is before me, but Joanna
Graia. Her sister, Lady Mary *Grey*, wrote Mary *Graye*, as
may be seen in her autograph, in Mr. Burgon's new work on
The Life and Times of Sir Thomas Gresham. So also their
cousin, Sir Henry *Grey* of Pirgo usually wrote his name Henry
Gray. Yet Sir Frederick would hardly recommend that the
accustomed form of writing the name of these historical personages
should be changed from *Grey* to *Gray* or *Graye*. When Lady

But the date in the title-page of that book is
1603, and no earlier edition is known.   How, then,
can this use have been made of the passage in a
play written in 1596?

There are two ways of evading this difficulty.
First, though we know of no earlier edition of this
translation (and it is improbable that there is any
earlier edition of it as a whole), it is by no means
improbable that a portion of it may have appeared
some years before in one of the smaller tracts of
Florio, of which there were many, more perhaps than
are now known to exist; and in that portion of it
the passage in question may have occurred.   Or,
secondly, this speech of Gonzalo's may have been

Jane was become the wife of Lord Guilford Dudley, she wrote
the name *Duddley* or *Duddeley*, for there are instances of both;
yet we are not, I suppose, about to transform the well known
name into one thus overburdened with consonants.   The other
point, which it seems to me has been overlooked, is this: that in
the time of Shakespeare there was the utmost indifference in
respect of the orthography of proper names, in writing especially,
but even in printing also.   Thus there is, as we have seen,
variety in the very few signatures which remain of Lady Jane
Dudley.   Of the name Shakespeare itself there are at least ten
or twelve various forms in which it was written during the Poet's
lifetime.   We have *Driden* and *Dryden*.   There are two title-
pages to the *Miscellanea Spiritualia* of Walter Montague, in
one of which the name of the author is *Montagu*, in the other
Mountague.   Sir Walter Raleigh, sometimes at least, wrote his
name *Rawley*.   The rule in this point, as in many others per-
taining to language, is the *usage* of persons of cultivation.   That
if we had more autographs from the Poet's own hand, we should
find that he allowed himself to write the name in various ortho-
graphies, it may seem unreasonable to presume.   But in the title-
pages of the few writings printed by him the name is *Shakespear*
or *Shakespeare*.   It is so in the titles of the quartos, in the titles
of the folios, and on the monument at Stratford.   It is so written
and printed by Camden, Jonson, Milton, and Dryden.   When
Jonson wrote
          " My Shakespear rise !"

added after the original appearance of the play, as
there is reason to think was the practice of Shakespeare. Alterations he certainly made from time to
time. As in *The Merry Wives of Windsor*, a reply
of Pistol was once,

" I will retort the sum in equipage ;"

and afterwards :

" Why then the world's mine oyster,
Which I with sword will open."

In a passage of *Hamlet*, we have three readings, all
indisputably Shakespeare's, namely, " godly ballad,"
" pious chanson," and that expression which has
been so ill explained by the commentators, " pons
chanson."*   In both these plays there have also

---

we feel at once that he could never have intended that the name
should be pronounced as the new orthography suggests; and
Green's pun upon the name, in that singularly curious notice of
him, which is his first introduction in the printed literature of
England, so far as is at present known, becomes greatly weakened
by the proposed change.

    Persons have acquiesced in the removal of the medial *e* without
sufficient consideration. There are authorities, ancient and modern, quite sufficient for retaining it, and we have thus an orthography which is nearer to the original elements. The name
classes with *Breakspear, Shakeshaft, Wagstaff*, and *Drawsword*,
of which name there was a lord mayor of York. They are a class
for which it is difficult to account. I conceive that the name was
pronounced with the first syllable sharp and short, *Shakspear*,
among his Stratford friends, but that in the polite society of
London he was Mr. *Shakespear*.

    The question deserved a note long as this; and the rather, be-
cause Mr. Knight has adopted this new orthography in his widely
circulated and highly embellished edition.

    * *Pons chansons*, says Pope, are *ballads sung on bridges ;* at
which the succeeding commentators smile, but suggest nothing
better.   In fact, a *pons chanson* is a trivial ballad, and the term
probably originated in such trifles being exposed to sale on the
Pont Neuf.—See the *Dictionnaire Historique des Mœurs*, &c.
Paris, 8vo. 1767. vol i. p. 417.

H

been large additions made after the work had been
deemed complete. As *Othello* existed in 1602, the
passage about the new heraldry of hands not hearts
must have been superinduced, if it allude to the red
hand of Ulster, which was given as an augmentation
to the members of the new order of baronets; and
this can hardly be doubted. It might, then, be said
that this passage, in which we have words of Florio,
was superinduced some time after the play was publicly performed.

But I propose to meet the difficulty, and not to
evade it. It is true that no printed edition of this
translation, or of any part of it, is known of an
earlier date than 1603. But it is also certain that
the translation was made several years before; for
as early as 1599, license was granted to Edward
Blount for the printing of it.† And for proof that
this is not the earliest period to which we can trace
this translation, I have only to refer you to the
Essays of Sir William Cornwallis, where you will
find not only that the translation was made, but that
it was divulged before that time. The first edition
of these Essays, indeed, bears date only in 1600;
but they were written some time before, for Henry
Olney, a friend of the author, under whose care they
were printed, assigns as the reason for publishing an
authentic edition, that copies were in so many hands,
there was danger lest the work might be printed by
some dishonest person surreptitiously. How much
time is to be allowed for this multiplication of copies
in manuscript, and for the original composition of
the Essays, it is impossible to estimate with much

---

† Herbert's Ames, No. 1383.

exactness; but it may fairly be allowed to conjecture that three or four years may have passed, which brings us near to the date we have assigned to *The Tempest*. But in what year soever Cornwallis wrote his Essays, in or before that year had Florio made his translation of Montaigne. For thus writes the author:

> "For profitable recreation that noble French knight, the Lord de Montaigne, is most excellent; whom, though I have not been so much beholding to the French as to see in his original, yet divers of his pieces I have seen translated, they that understand both languages say very well done; and I am able to say (if you will take the word of ignorance) translated into a style admitting as few idle words as our language will endure. It is well fitted in this new garment, and Montaigne speaks now good English. It is done by a fellow less beholding to nature for his fortune than wit, yet lesser for his face than his fortune: the truth is, he looks more like a good fellow than a wise man; and yet he is wise beyond either his fortune or education."

Florio's profession was that of a French and Italian master, in which he was the most eminent man of his time; and the portions of Montaigne in an English translation, to which Cornwallis alludes, may be supposed with likelihood enough to have been prepared by him for the use of his scholars.

But being seen by Cornwallis, is it too violent a presumption that they may have been seen by Shakespeare also, especially as the Florios, for there were two, Michael-Angelo and John, were noticed by the Herberts from the time when Michael-Angelo dedicated a work, now in manuscript in the Public Library at Cambridge, to Henry, Earl of Pembroke, in 1553, to the time of the death of John Florio, in 1625, who leaves his corrections of the Italian dictionary published by him, to William, Earl of Pem-

broke,* whose connection with Shakespeare is so
remarkable a circumstance in the history of both.

Shakespeare is even brought into immediate connection with Florio sometime before the date which
I have assigned to *The Tempest*. I shall not repeat
the argument of Bishop Warburton to prove that
Florio is ridiculed in the *Love Labours Lost*, under
the character of Holofernes, nor enter now into the
question whether he is so or no. But I would observe that, supposing it was the intention of Shakespeare, for whatever reason, and it must have been a
reason arising in the private relations between them,
to hold up Florio to ridicule in that play, it is done,
not in the character of Holofernes the schoolmaster
taken singly, but Holofernes and Armado together make up John Florio. The proofs are indeed pregnant; for Florio, though undoubtedly he
deserved well of the country that adopted him, and
was perhaps a main instrument in introducing Italian
writers to the notice of Englishmen, which did so
much to raise the character of our literature and
poetry, was in truth a somewhat vain, pedantic,
and thrasonical person. However, without going
further into this question,† I think I have said suf-

---

* This I gathered from his Will, a document of some interest,
which I have perused at Doctors' Commons. These corrections
are said, I know not how justly, to have been used by Torriano.
What treasures for the illustration of our literary history may not
the archives of such families as the Herberts, Sidneys, Russells,
Sackviles, Percys, contain ; but the enlargement of the knowledge
we possess of the men of the Elizabethan and later periods is
chiefly to be expected from the testamentary documents preserved
in the ecclesiastical courts.

† The passage quoted from Cornwallis contains a singular
allusion to something that was peculiar in the *face* of Florio.
It will be remembered that Jaquenetta, in *Love Labours Lost*,

ficient to shew that Shakespeare may not improbably have seen portions of Florio's Montaigne in 1596. I must now dispose of Mr. Chalmers' dead Indian. When Trinculo, in ridicule of the passion of Englishmen for seeing sights shewn to them by travellers, says, " When they will not give a doit to relieve a lame beggar, they will lay out ten to see a dead Indian," Mr. Chalmers tells us that he alludes to a circumstance which occurred as late as the year 1611. In that year the Earl of Southampton and Sir Francis Gorges brought to England five Indians, four of whom left England alive some time after. Mr. Chalmers adds, " We may easily suppose of the other that he died in London, and was exhibited for a show." Undoubtedly we may : but evidence exists that an Indian died in London many years before, and, not indeed that his body was exhibited for a

---

makes a retort to Armado, which is hardly intelligible : " With that face ?" May this be taken as any kind of evidence that Florio is in that play ?

At the same time I see nothing peculiar in the visage of Florio as it appears in the engraved portrait before his *Queen Anna's New World of Words.*

There was an original portrait of him in the possession of the Dorset family, by Mytens, which, if existing, might shew what Cornwallis meant. It is not named in the printed catalogue of the paintings at Knole, where are some portraits that are anonymous, but it is mentioned in a remarkable manuscript at the Museum, No. 4636, of the Harleian Library, of which I cannot find that any use has ever been made ; and yet it contains much of the private thoughts of no less a person than the Earl of Dorset, who was the friend and patron of Dryden, on many very important subjects, chiefly political, written by his own hand. The manuscript is anonymous, and the catalogue gives no intimation of the author. The indications of the hand from which it came are, however, I think, sufficiently plain. We have this judgment upon Shakespeare ; " None ever made the saying of Cicero's good so well as Shakespeare, that *Ingenii bonitas sæpe imitatur doctrinam.*"

show, but that a wax model of his body was made after his death, no doubt for the purpose of being publicly exhibited. This unfortunate being, the account of whose capture cannot be read without a strong feeling of indignation against so unfeeling a use of that higher power which civilization gives, was brought to England by Frobisher, in 1577. In the accounts of the expenses of that voyage, which have been printed by the late commissioners on the public records,* whose works assist in enquiries in the grander subjects of historical research, and in the lighter literature of such a work as this, the following entry occurs :—

" Paid William Cure, Ducheman, graver, for making a mould of hard earth of the Tartar man's image, to be cast in wax."

The body itself was embalmed and deposited in a coffin.

I am not aware that there is any other difficulty, or any other subsidiary or corroborative argument to the main argument, produced by Mr. Malone or Mr. Chalmers, which requires consideration.

---

* *Proceedings of the Board of Commissioners on the Public Records*, folio 1834, p. 75. The passage in the account of the capture of this unfortunate man, to which there is allusion in the text, is this :—" Whereupon, when he found himself in captivity, for very choler and disdain he bit his tongue in twain within his mouth: notwithstanding, he died not thereof, but lived until he came to England, and then he died of cold which he had taken at sea." I quote from the Variorum, vol. xii., p. 96, an extract from an account of Frobisher's First Voyage for the Discovery of Cataya, 4to., 1578.

VI.

ORIGIN OF THE PLOT AND PRINCIPAL CHARACTERS.

I TRUST that I may at length have succeeded in establishing the following points: that *The Tempest* is one of the earlier works of Shakespeare, having been written by him in the spring or summer of the year 1596, when he was thirty-two years of age: that in the composition of it he had particularly in view the ridiculous stories contained in the pamphlet of Sir Walter Raleigh, published in that year, and the correction of what was likely to become a dangerous popular delusion: that the island of Bermuda had nothing to do with the idea formed in his mind of a deserted, stormy, and enchanted island, but that the archetype from which he wrought was the island of Lampedusa, situated not far from the northern coast of Africa: that the island of Lampedusa not only suggested to him, as Bermuda has heretofore been supposed to have done, some of the minuter circumstances of the desert island on which he has laid the scene of this play, but that the island is in fact the scene where all the incidents of the play take place, and was intended to be so regarded by the Poet: that he owed nothing to the pamphlet of Sil. Jourdan, in which we have an account of the wreck of Sir George Somers and Sir Thomas Gates on the coast of Bermuda, the play having been written many years before the time of that accident: and that when he delineated the storm in the first and second scenes, he had in his mind, and to a certain extent used, the noble description of a storm at sea in the forty-first canto of Ariosto, using for this purpose the translation of Sir John Harington.

All these are, I believe, *novelties* in Shakespeare criticism, and I venture to think that they will be found of some importance; that they will in fact work a great revolution in the criticism on this play, both as respects the play as a whole, and as respects particular scenes and passages in it. Certain it is, that if these views are just, much of the present prolegomena, and many of the present notes may be withdrawn, and other prolegomena and other annotation must take their place.

I have hitherto brought under your notice very little in three distinct departments of Shakespeare criticism : the developement of origins of the plots and more marked characters ; the explanation of obsolete words or obscure passages ; and the proper regulation of a text which has come down to us in a very corrupted state, and which, to say the least, has not yet been fully and happily restored. In each of these departments I have a few observations to make on this play.

And first, on the origin of the plot and of the three most remarkable characters in it, Prospero, Ariel, and Caliban.

In the search after the originals on which Shakespeare worked in the composition of his dramas, much diligence has been used by the commentators, and with no little success.

Some object to these inquiries, as if they tend but to the derogation of Shakespeare. But it is a great mistake to suppose that researches of this kind have

been conducted with a view to lessen his claim to
originality, or to any other quality which we admire
in a writer. It is enough to say that they have
been conducted by the fondest and most devoted of
his admirers, who have thought themselves supremely
happy if they could trace the footsteps of Shakespeare in any corner of the field of European literature, where no one had before suspected that he had
trod. There is no room to suspect treachery or treason. Their single aim has been to do homage to
Shakespeare, by leaving nothing unattempted which
may by possibility throw light on anything which
he has written, or the antecedent working in his own
mind. This seems to me to be homage of the best
kind, the most unexceptionable evidence of the
Poet's greatness.

But do we, in point of fact, by researches such as
these, lose any particle of the admiration in which
we hold him? Who values *Romeo and Juliet* the
less, because he knows that the story is to be found
in Painter and Brooke? or *Othello*, because it is a
tale of Cynthio's? Do we esteem *As You Like It*
the less, when we have read the Rosalinde of Lodge?
or will *Twelfth Night* afford us less pleasure, or be
less the object of high admiration, because we now
find that the plot has a near resemblance to that of
the *Ingannati* of an Italian academy? If we found
that the moonlight scene in *The Merchant of Venice*
exhibits traces of his reading in Chaucer, should we
read it with a less exquisite delight, or discern in it
less clearly a hand that is incomparable?

The comparison of the story as he found it, and
the story as he made it, is also one of the most agree-
able occupations in the study of Shakespeare. And

here I cannot but draw your attention to the beautiful works of Mr. Augustine Skottowe, too little read, in which the most experienced student in Shakespeare will find many most valuable remarks.

But if it is still maintained, that it is treason against the majesty of Shakespeare to say, that he did not invent his own plots, and that he took suggestion occasionally in the details of his works, still there is a satisfaction in knowing what is the real fact; and there is a love of truth, as well as a love of Shakespeare, and a homage due unto both.

The origin of the plot of the *The Tempest* is for the present a Shakesperian mystery; and I must at once confess, that little that is important has presented itself in the course of my researches. Have you, in your cabinet of Shakespeare curiosities, the rare volume that would make all clear?

That the plot of *The Tempest* has an origin in something out of the mind of the Poet himself, I regard as unquestionable: that is, that there existed previously to the composition of this play some story or drama in which was the deposition of Prospero, his residence in a desert island, and his recognition there with an unworthy brother, whom an accident had thrown upon its shores, together with more or less of the subordinate incidents, the marriage of Claribel, and the marriage of Miranda, and more or less of the magic and enchantment of the piece. It is clear that Shakespeare must have had some other information of the qualities of the isle of Lampedusa than he could gain from Ariosto or from Crusius, and it would be extremely difficult to shew how that knowledge was acquired, except

from some such writer as one who had devised a tale
of which that island was the scene.   Beside, when
of the six and thirty plays we find that all, with the
exception of *The Tempest* and one other, are formed
upon stories, dramas, or pieces of history which before existed, the probability is that the two excepted
had like origins, though, with the wide field of the
romantic and dramatic literature of Europe before us,
those origins have not yet been detected.

The origin of one other play beside *The Tempest*
has not yet been discovered.   I pray you to remark
which of the plays it is.   It is the *Love Labours
Lost*, to which an old title of *The Tempest* (if I am
right in that part of the preceding argument) was
respondent, *Love Labours Won*.   The two plays
thus may be said to hang together; but they have
this more remarkable circumstance common to both:
in those plays, and in no other of the romantic
dramas, have we characters and events of real history.   They are strangely altered, blended, and per-
verted, but still in both plays we have a certain
reference to the veritable facts and persons of modern
European history, and are able to fix chronological
periods to which the incidents of the plot are to be
referred.   If in respect of any other of the romantic
dramas we ask the question, " Under which king,
Bezonian ?" the answer must be, We cannot tell.
Not so with *The Tempest* and *Love Labours Lost*.

From this I infer that there is some one book to
which Shakespeare had recourse for the plots of
both these plays : a book of romances (or possibly,
but less probably, a book of dramas), in which the
stories were offsets from the events of genuine his-

tory, or those events mingled with fictions, the creations of the author's mind ; and that therefore these
two plays do form but in fact one exception to the
rule that Shakespeare, we know, wrought on plots
prepared to his hand.

That the *Love Labours Lost* had an origin in a
previous romance, though the romance cannot be
now produced, will hardly be doubted by any one
who shall read attentively the long speech about
the Aquitaine bond, in which we see the Poet not
expressing his own free thoughts, but struggling to
exhibit in verse the intractable matter of a money
contract as another had previously exhibited it in
prose.

I would further submit, that the story of *The
Tempest*, as well as that of *Love Labours Lost*, has
not an English air, but is more like a production of
the romance writers of the sixteenth century of France
or Italy, Navarre or Spain.

And here, allow me to ask how it has happened
that the critics abroad, and especially those of Ger-
many, who are such great admirers of Shakespeare,
have done nothing for us in this department? We
know of books printed in our own country, which
exist but at present in single copies : may we not,
therefore, presume that this may be the case with
books printed abroad, so that it is not wonderful that
the books are unknown in England? Story books
are perhaps, more than books of any other description, liable to this extinction, owing to the attraction
which they present to children, in whose hands books
soon perish. I would suggest to the lovers of Shakespeare on the continent, that search should be made
in the libraries for rare books of this class in the

literature of the sixteenth century, and that a better service could scarcely be rendered in bibliography, than to bring to light the rarer volumes of this rare class, and to make known what particular stories they contain.

But after all, there is the possibility that the stories which Shakespeare here used, never reached the press, but were circulated in manuscript copies. Painter, if I recollect right, had collected many more stories than he has printed.

In the absence of the true origin, the most improbable suppositions have been promulgated. A play of Green's, and a tale of Turbervile's have been propounded. Even the history of Aurelio and Isabella has been spoken of. I have a copy of this rare book, which belongs to the class of philosophical romances. Isabella is a daughter of a certain King of Scotland. It has been already observed, that the story has no resemblance whatever to that of *The Tempest*. What the ballad of which Mr. Collier speaks,* may turn out, remains to be seen. A question will arise upon it, whether the ballad or the play is the earlier work. Nothing could be easier than to construct a story out of the incidents of the play.

I have said that the story and characters of *The Tempest*, have a certain relation to events and personages in the history of modern Europe. Thus there was a real Alonzo, King of Naples, who had a son named Ferdinand, who succeeded him in his kingdom in 1495. Ferdinand did not, as in the play, marry a princess of the house of Milan, but the two

---

* *New Particulars regarding the Works of Shakespeare,* 8vo. 1836, p. 46.

houses were, at that time, united by the marriage of
Alonzo himself with Hippolita Sforza, a daughter of
Francis the First, Duke of Milan. Ferdinand died
young, and was succeeded by an uncle, who bore, however, the name of Ferdinand, and not Sebastian as in
the play. Then turning to the history of Milan, we
have a banished duke who was dispossessed in 1514,
by Francis the First of France. We have also an
usurping Duke of Milan, corresponding to Anthonio,
in a brother of Maximilian. To the banished duke, he
who first constructed the story, seems to have given
attributes which belong to Alonzo, King of Naples, of
whom it is reported (I quote the words of our own
countryman, William Thomas, in his *History of Italy*,
4to. 1549), that he " renounced the estate unto his son
(Ferdinand), took his treasure with him, and sailed
into Sicily; where, for the time of his short life, that
dured scarce one year, he disposed himself to study,
solitariness, and religion." But Francis, Duke of
Milan, himself, may seem to have had a taste for the
studies in which Prospero was so accomplished an
adept; for I have a treatise on witchcraft, printed at
Milan in 1490, in which the reality of the whole of
what goes under the name of magic is affirmed, and
the book is dedicated to this Duke by its author,
Jerome Visconti. The name Prospero does not occur
in either family, but it may have been suggested by
the name of the celebrated commander, Prospero
Colonna, who had much to do in all the affairs of
the Milanese during the troubles. You see, therefore, that the person who constructed this story, had
in his mind the members of the two houses of Naples
and Milan, at the time when those ancient sovereign-
ties were fast hastening to their fall; and that there-

fore there is no occasion to go to such collections as the *Gesta* for the origin of this story, or to dive for it into the depths of the imaginative literature of modern Europe. It is clearly a story comparatively of recent origin, probably not older than the middle of the sixteenth century, some time being required to prepare veritable persons of history, even when thus wildly disguised, for the purposes of romance. It is probable that it was written even after the time when the island was sacked by the Algerines under Barbarossa. The era of the action in *Love Labours Lost*, may be more precisely fixed to about the year 1428.

There is a passage in the second scene of the first act, which shews an intimate acquaintance with Italian affairs, perhaps not more intimate than may justly be attributed to Shakespeare himself, the extent and variety of whose knowledge is not the least extraordinary part of his wonderful character. The passage is corrupted in the first fólio, not properly restored in the second, and given as in the first by the modern editors. I read thus :

> " as, at that time,
> Though [of] all the seignories it was the first,
> And Prospero the prime Duke (being so reputed
> In dignity), and for the liberal arts
> Without a parallel."

Prospero is speaking of the Duchy of Milan, of which Botero says, " Milan claims to be the first Duchy in Europe."* The University of Pavia was in high reputation.

With the plot are interwoven many of the de-

---

* *Relations of the most famous Kingdoms and Commonweulths*, 4to. 1630, p. 337 : but there is an earlier edition.

tails of a species of philosophy of very remote origin, and which prevailed to a great extent throughout Europe in the middle ages, and for many years after the period which is often called, rightly or wrongly, the revival of letters. It had its origin in the East. Solomon was a great adept. So, long before his time, were Jannes and Jambres who withstood Moses. The three Magi who made the offerings when guided by a star to Bethlehem, were persons of the same class. So was Simon Magus: and so were the magicians who burnt their books when the Apostle witnessed against such vanities. The Chaldæans and the Chaldaic arts, of which we read in the Roman authors, belong to this philosophy. The traditions or imaginations of the middle ages, assigned to Virgil an eminent place among those who cultivated it. There are then a crowd of persons in the countries of modern Europe, and especially about all the shores of the Mediterranean, who were more or less dupes or professors of this so-called philosophy. I find little of it, however, in its pure state in England. Our superstitions of the kind have a nearer affinity to those of the North of Europe, from whence we come. Our persons of this class are rather necromancers than pure magicians, though the two characters would, no doubt, often run into each other. Ours was rather the Black Magic, or the Black Art, more properly so called, than the White Magic, which is that of *The Tempest.**

---

* The commentators speak of Dr. John Dee, as if this eminent philosopher, in the twilight of modern science, were a kind of actual Prospero. But it seems due to the memory of a man to whom English science owes such important obligations, and of whom I could almost say, that he deserves to be placed in the

The professors of the species of philosophy of which I speak, pretended to be able to perform very

---

first rank of great men whom this island has produced, and would probably, by universal suffrage, have been so placed if he had been born later than the time of Bacon, if not to take him out of their hands, yet to hint a serious doubt whether he has not been greatly misunderstood.   Certain it is, that he has this eloquent passage in his preface to the Euclid: " And for these and such like marvellous acts and feats, naturally, mathematically, and mechanically wrought and contrived, ought any honest student and modest Christian enquirer be counted and called a 𝕮𝖔𝖓𝖏𝖚𝖗𝖊𝖗? Shall the folly of idiots, and the malice of the scornful so much prevail, that he who seeketh no worldly gain or glory at their hands, but only of God the treasurer of heavenly wisdom and knowledge of pure verity : shall he, I say, in the mean space, be robbed and spoiled of his honest name and fame ? He that seeketh, by Saint Paul's advertisement, in the creatures, properties and wonderful virtues, to find just cause to glorify the Eternal and Almighty Creator by : shall that man be in hugger-mugger condemned, as a companion of the hell-hounds, and a caller and conjurer of wicked and damned spirits ?"   This was written from his " poor house at Mortlake, anno 1590, February 9." Will the name of Dee again appear as a counter-part of Prospero ?

It is enough to awaken a high respect to peruse some of the remains of this eminent person in the Cottonian Manuscripts. They shew a devotedness to science, properly so called, of which the world has seen too few examples. He is also eminently among the unfortunate learned. He went before his age : and he eclipsed too many persons by the superiority of his acquirements.   His life ought to be written in a manner very different from that in which it has been hitherto delivered to us.   It should be the work of one in whose mind is the rare combination of the spirit of close literary research, an intimate acquaintance with the state of European science in the time of Dee, and in the century before, and the ability to take a philosophical view of the evidence, and all the facts of his extraordinary case.   Who is sufficient for this ?   I think I see rising among us one who is so :

" Macte novâ virtute puer."

When such an attempt is made, the testimony of Nash must not be overlooked, which is found in his *Christ's Tears over Jerusalem*, 1593.   " Under Master Dee's name, the like fabulous divinations have been bruited ; when, good reverend old man ! he is as far from any such arrogant prescience, as the superstitious spreaders of it are from peace of conscience." P. 90[b].

1

extraordinary feats. They deluded the senses of sight, hearing, and taste, and seemed to satisfy, though with nothing, the cravings of hunger. They triumphed over time and space. They knew men's thoughts. They could make the very elements obey them. This they professed to do, not by any power inherent in themselves, but by the instrumentality of spiritual agents, whom they had in their control: fallen angels they were, who had lost their first estate, and who were shut up in stocks and stones of the earth, from which, however, they might be evoked by those who knew the *call*.

Prospero is an impersonation of these adepts. We see his power over the elements, his intimacy with the thoughts and purposes of other men, the splendid visions, the aerial music, the unreal banquets: and we see him with the robes, the wand, and the books, which were the constant adjuncts of the character of which he is the impersonation.

No doubt, feats which, in a less enlightened age, baffled the less imperfect philosophy of the common people, were performed by the persons who professed this art. There might be among the original spectators of this play, some who believed in the power of such men to produce the delusive visions and the aerial music which fill so large a space in it; as there are still who believe in the reality of such appearances as the ghosts of Banquo and of the father of Hamlet. I shall give some particular instances of these delusions at the close of this section.

To what book Shakespeare resorted for his information on this point, which appears to have been minute and critical, has never been shewn. The book which would most naturally present itself was

The Discovery of Witchcraft, by that shrewd and sensible old writer, Reginald Scot, which was published in 1584. The fifteenth book of that work relates to this branch of the subject; but I do not trace Shakespeare anywhere in it.

I am even doubtful whether traces can be found in any of the plays, that Shakespeare read this work, although it fell in remarkably with his own just and rational views on all subjects connected with the superstitions of the age. Scot, for instance, has a long roll of spirits, name by name, who served the adepts in the art, with their several seignories and degrees, their shapes, powers, government, and effects. It is a very remarkable chapter; an extraordinary exhibition of human folly and vanity. But when Shakespeare had a spirit to name, he adopts not one of the names which are to be found in Scot; Baell, Agares, Zopar, Paimon, Procel, Amy, Allocer, or the hundred others, but either invents a name not before in the spiritual vocabulary, or adopts one from the undiscovered writer whom he follows. The name is ARIEL, the Lion of God, a word of Hebrew origin, classing with Raphael, Gabriel, Michael, and other names of the angelic host. In the dramatis personæ, Ariel is described as " an airy spirit;" and the resemblance in the sound of the word to this description, was perhaps the sole circumstance which determined Shakespeare to the choice, if it were a choice, and not an invention. But having chosen or invented the name, there is reason to think that he resorted to that part of the prophet Isaiah, in which this word is used as a personation of Jerusalem, and some of the attributes and feats of Ariel may seem to have been suggested by what he read in the prophet.

Mr. Douce has already pointed out the resemblance, but it may not be inexpedient to draw attention again to coincidences which, if coincidences only, are somewhat remarkable. Thus, of the Scripture Ariel, it is said, " Thy speech shall be low out of the dust : thy voice shall be as of one that hath a familiar spirit : thy speech shall whisper out of the dust." Here we seem to have the airy tongues, the voices which are heard when no one is visible.—" Thou shalt be visited with thunder and with earthquake, and great noise; with storm and tempest, and the flames of devouring fire." The play is full of these through the instrumentality of Ariel. The next is more critical :—" It shall even be as when an hungry man dreameth, and behold he eateth ; but he awaketh, and his soul is empty : or as when a thirsty man dreameth, and behold he drinketh." Compare with this the unreal banquets which Ariel prepares :— " The Lord hath poured on you the spirit of deep sleep, and hath closed your eyes." Hence, perhaps, the artificial drowsiness, and the deep slumber which Ariel is represented as inducing : and, finally, when the prophet, in his sublime poetry, says, " And the multitude of all the nations that fight against Ariel, even all that fight against her and her munition, and that distress her, shall be as a dream of a night vision ;" we have perhaps the germ of a very celebrated passage in this drama, the beauty of which is more impressively felt when we recollect that the words were spoken by Prospero in the very hour when the machinations against his life were to have taken effect :   .

" We are such stuff
As dreams are made of, and our little life
Is rounded by a sleep."   *Act* iv. *Sc.* 1.

As Prospero is a personation of the adepts, so is Ariel a personation of the spirits; his form, dimensions, properties, such as flying, swimming, passing through fire, riding on the clouds, are all such as belonged, or were supposed to belong to the spirits of whom we speak, whether they were

" Elves of *hills, brooks, standing lakes,* or *groves,*"

or of the *sea-shore* or of *meadows,* who are indicated in the beautiful and well-remembered periphrases: but the spirits of air seem to have possessed some of the properties in a higher degree than the somewhat grosser spirits of the earth. Prospero is made to describe the powers belonging to them. It was by their aid that he had bedimmed the noontide sun, produced the tempest which had placed his enemies in his power: lightning, thunder, and earthquake had been their work. Whatever else that was preternatural was produced by their agency. Ariel represents them all : and when he is represented as having been punished by a witch, freed by Prospero, bound to serve him, uneasy in the service, longing for liberty, we are to regard these characteristics of Ariel but as an instance of there being given to one individual attributes which belonged to the whole tribe to which he belonged.

The address to these spirits by Prospero at the beginning of the fifth act, which is coloured with all the rainbow tints of Shakespeare's fine imagination, is called an *invocation* by Mr. Steevens. I do not regard it in that light. It is an address, but not intended as a *call.* The call, at least as applied to Ariel, is very peculiar; and yet the peculiarity has not, I think, been observed. It resembles the call which

may be used to a bird of paradise, or of a mistress
to her favourite sparrow:

> " Come away, servant, come : I am ready now:
> Approach, my Ariel; come."   *Act* i. *Sc.* 2.

And again :

> " Now, come my Ariel :—appear, and pertly."
> *Act* iv. *Sc.* 1.

And again :

> " Come with a thought :—Ariel, come." *Act* iv. *Sc.* 1.

The call is introduced on other occasions, and is
always in perfect harmony with the delicate form of
Ariel, in which the idea of a bee, perhaps, rather
predominates than that of any other living thing.
But Mr. Steevens has a misapprehension respecting
this celebrated address, of a more serious kind.
Having spoken of it as an invocation, he wonders
what the spirits were to do if they came when Prospero called for them : " Yet to what purpose they
were invoked does not very distinctly appear." The
purpose was this ; to hear the announcement which
Prospero makes, that he has abjured all future com-
merce with them. They were not to *come forth* to
hear this. The words of Prospero conveying this
announcement was to enter their ears in whatever
cell they might be concealed. This was the purpose
of the address, and unless we distinctly apprehend
it as the purpose, the lines, beautiful as they are,
will be but *nugæ canoræ, versus inopes rerum ;* but
when this their real purpose is understood, they become an essential part of the drama.

> " But this rough magic
> I here abjure : and when I have requir'd
> Some heavenly music . . . I'll break my staff;
> Bury it certain fathoms in the earth ;

And, deeper than did ever plummet sound,
I'll drown my book."

Shakespeare has preserved the unities of action, place and time. It was a great day in the life of all the parties who are conspicuous in the story; and not the least important incident is, that it was the day when Prospero renounced his " secret studies," and determined to devote himself for the remainder of his life to studies not forbidden, or to the thoughts which would naturally spring out of the retrospect of a life full of such strange accidents. Of how many other persons it was a. day ever to be remembered, by some with joy and delight, by others with confusion and shame, it is unnecessary to speak.

The progress of the affection of Ferdinand and Miranda, including the obstructions thrown in their way by Prospero, is the only part of the story which, without any violation of probability, we may not suppose to have taken place within the limits of time assigned in the drama. All the other events might well occur within the six or eight hours to which the time is confined. But the love which we are to regard as being an affection springing up at the same moment in the breasts of both, when first accident has thrown them in the way of each other, we are also to regard as quickened by the influence of enchantment: and after all, it is little more than what we see in the two lovers of Verona, and approve there as being true to nature.

There is much of what is Hebraistic in this play. Did you ever observe how like to the manner of the ancient Jews is the mode in which time is measured in the following lines?

" She that is Queen of Tunis; she that dwells
Ten leagues beyond man's life; she, that from Naples
Can have no note, unless the sun were post,
(The man i' th' moon's too slow) *till new born chins
Be rough and razorable*."   *Act* ii. *Sc.* 1.

In the expression, " ten leagues beyond man's
life," a critic whom I formerly knew, and who printed a pamphlet of Shakespeare annotation scarcely
known to the most inveterate Shakesperians, and
yet containing better matter than some more pre-
tending works,* finds another scriptural allusion,
referring it to the affecting words of the ninetieth
psalm, respecting the age of man. The explanation
of our late friend Dr. Sherwen was, " ten leagues

---

* *Annotations on Plays of Shakespeare,* York, 8vo., 1810.—
This pamphlet consists of twenty-four closely printed pages, and I
venture to say contains more valuable remark than is to be found in
the volumes of Zachary Jackson, and Andrew Becket, or even those
of John Lord Chedworth, and Henry James Pye. The author was
Mr. John Croft, who had published, in 1792, another pamphlet, which
belongs to this subject, which he entitled *A Select Collection of
the Beauties of Shakspear, with some account of his Life*: but
this is worthless. There are a few other tracts of his, one of
which is entitled *Excerpta Antiqua*, and another, *A Treatise on
the Wines of Portugal*, in the title of which he describes himself
as " John Croft, s. A. s., Member of the Factory at Oporto, and
wine merchant, York." The time may perhaps come, when the
names of all persons who have published distinct tracts in illustration of Shakespeare, or who have contributed to the notes in
variorum editions, will be gathered together, and some account
be given of them, with a discrimination, which is greatly wanted,
of the peculiar character of the contribution which each has
offered at Shakespeare's shrine : when it will be of some service
to be informed that Mr. Croft was a member of a family of distinction in the county of York; that he resided many years at
Oporto ; and that when he returned to England he became settled
at York, where he had a house, with gardens extending to the
ramparts, between Monk Bar and Laythorpe Postern : that his
personal appearance was singularly grotesque ; a figure made by
one of Nature's journeymen, was usually invested in a dress half

beyond the line of human habitation."* Neither is satisfactory, though as good as Mr. Steevens's, which alone is found in the Variorum : " At a greater distance than the life of man is long enough to reach." Shall I hazard a conjecture ; though my guess at the solution of this Ælia Lelia Crispis may be as little satisfactory as the rest ? But may not *man's life* in this place, like *The Place of Depth†* in *The Comedy of Errors*, be the name of some African city " done into English." *Romeo and Juliet* supplies us with an instance of this kind of translation, where we have " *Old Free Town*," as the name of an Italian city. Such translation proceeded on an erroneous

---

English, half Portuguese : but under this exterior, there was a certain kind of elegance, and when I knew him, an extraordinary avidity for information, especially historical and Shakesperian. He was a great questionist, and every third question which he asked was *Unde derivatur ?* It seems to have been his habit to put down in his note-book at home, whatever anecdotes or criticisms he could collect in his walks abroad. He was to be seen at every book auction, where his biddings were regulated by a strict regard to economy ; and if met in the streets, the chance was that to his outré figure was to be added, that he had an Elizabethan quarto under his arm. He died about the year 1812, and what became of his books or manuscript notes I never heard.

* The notes of Dr. Sherwen here alluded to are in two quarto volumes, which he left in a manuscript, to which he gave the title *Vindicatio Shakesperiana.* The manuscript was given, after his decease, to the library of the Royal Institution at Bath, where it is now deposited.

† The reader will look in vain for this " place of depth" in any of the common editions of Shakespeare. By an alteration, the most injudicious and unjustifiable, this, the genuine reading, has been made to give way to a poor and weak expression, and we now read,

" Anon, I am sure the Duke himself in person
Comes this way to the melancholy vale,
The place of *death* and sorry execution,
Behind the ditches of the Abbey here."   *Act* v. *Sc.* 1.

principle, but it was a principle of the time.   I give
it only as a conjecture, but if it should prove a sound
conjecture, the inference will be unavoidable that
the story was originally told in some other language
than English.

More remarkable is it that CALIBAN seems in his
form to be of Hebraistic origin.   The peculiar, dis-
tinguishing, and indeed very remarkable character-
istic of the form is, that he is half-fish, half-man.
It has often been said that the form and functions of
Caliban are a pure creation of Shakespeare's own
mind; but I doubt it.   Did you ever compare him
with the *fish-idol* of Ashdod, the Dagon of the Philistines?

> " Sea-monster! upward man,
> And downward fish."   *P. L. Book* i. *Line* 462.

Here we have also a figure half-fish half-man.   But
such a Dagon as Milton has delineated could not do
what Caliban is represented as having done.   Milton,
however, had his choice of two forms of Dagon : for
it has been a question in Rabbinical literature how
the two elements of fish and man coalesced in the
form of Dagon.   Kimchi had represented the fish-
god of the Philistines in the manner in which Milton represents it.   Abarbinel, on the contrary, argued
from the obscure intimations which remain of this
strange conception, that Kimchi was mistaken, and
that the true form of Dagon was a figure, " shaped
like a fish, only with feet and hands like a man."*
Now this is precisely the form of Shakespeare's

---

* *Antiquities of the Hebrew Republic*, by Thomas Lewis, 8vo.
1724, vol. ii. p. 81.—Milton, it may be observed, though in the
Paradise Lost he had adopted Kimchi's form of the idol, which
till the time of Abarbinel had, perhaps, not been questioned, yet

Caliban, "a fish legged like a man, and his fins like arms." Nothing can be more precise than the resemblance. The two are in fact one, as to form. Caliban is therefore a kind of tortoise, the paddles expanding in arms and hands, legs and feet. And accordingly, before he appears upon the stage, the audience are prepared for the strange figure, by the words of Prospero:

"Come forth, thou *tortoise !*"

How he became changed into a monkey, while the play is full of allusions to his fish-like form, those who introduced the clothes-line may explain.

Steevens says, that there is no conceivable figure with which all the functions and actions of Caliban can be made to cohere. I do not agree with him. With the form which Shakespeare really gave to him, every thing is consistent.

The question then arises whether there being an existent prototype, we are warranted in going on affirming that Caliban is a being wholly of Shakespeare's own formation? Is it more probable that he imagined the form, or adopted it? That he gave it passions, voice, action of his own, every thing, in short, in which the merit consists, may be willingly allowed ; but it is scarcely probable that two minds in two distant countries and two distant ages of the world, should both have given birth to so unnatural a conception   If Shakespeare, writing for the stage, had been left at liberty to devise a monster for his story, he would not, I think, of his own accord, have

---

when he has to speak of Dagon again in the Samson Agonistes, he avoids assigning to it any particular figure :

" To-day a solemn feast the people hold
To Dagon, their sea-idol."

given it attributes so unmanageable on a stage as
those of a fish.

If it is asked where he gained his acquaintance
with the figure of Dagon, as delineated by Abarbinel, it might be answered in the emphatic expression
of Coleridge, ·that Shakespeare was " a myriad-
minded man :" there was no department of human
knowledge with which he had not some acquaintance.
I looked in vain for any speculations on the figure
of Dagon, in the Genevan Annotations, which were
doubtless often read by him. The probability is,
that he found the form of Caliban in that undiscovered story or drama, in which he found also Prospero and the white magic, and where also he found
Lampedusa, with its physical and metaphysical
attributes.

Light might possibly be thrown on Sycorax and
Caliban by a search in any early writers, if such
there be, who treat on the superstitions of Algiers
and the African coast.

One word more respecting Caliban. The origin
of the *name* is matter of uncertainty. Dr. Farmer's
conjecture may be the true one, that it is a meta-
thesis of Canibal ; Setebos, the name of the great
god of Sycorax and her son, being unquestionably an
Indian word. Dr. Sherwen thought that Caliban was
a hybrid word, compounded of *ban* and *beauty*.
Would it not be a circumstance deserving to be taken
notice of, if it should turn out that Caliban is one
among the many names by which the Three Magi
are known in different countries of Europe? Gaspar,
Melchior, and Balthazar, are the names by which
they are called most generally; but they are also
known by the names of Magalath, Galgalath, and
Sarasin ; Apellius, Amerus, and Damasus ; Ator,

Sator, and Paratoras. I have also seen Melchior, *Caliban*, and Mamamouchi ; but as it was in a book of no authority, and may have been intended for a burlesque, I shall say no more about it.

I promised that, before this section was closed, I would present you with some notices of the power which some persons in the middle ages possessed, of producing delusions of various kinds, resembling those which we find in this play. Chaucer has given a very lively description of what could be done by an accomplished tregetour. Persons seated in the great hall of a castle, saw a barge come sailing in, or a lion prowl about the room : suddenly the stone floor would become a green mead, in which sprung daisies and butter-cups ; a vine would be trailed along the wall, and grapes would appear in the little green bunches, which would soon be enlarged, coloured, and ripened. Chaucer tells us that he had actually seen this, possibly when he was abroad : but Aubrey, in a manuscript on Remains of Gentilism in the Superstitions and Customs of England, containing much curious matter, which is now in the Lansdowne Library, at the Museum, speaks of an exhibition resembling this, in a hall, near Dursley, at which his grandfather was present, in the reign of Henry the Eighth. John Melton, the author of that sensible tract, The Astrologaster, describes an exhibition which he had himself witnessed at Cambridge, in the reign of James the First, in which an orange plant was seen to spring in the midst of a room, to grow up into a goodly tree, and finally to bear fruit which went on enlarging and ripening in the presence of the spectators.

We, who have witnessed the phantasmagoria and

the diorama, may conceive the possibility of decep-
tions such as these : though, I confess, it seems as if
in these dioptrical illusions there was greater skill
in former ages than is manifested in these times. As
little difficulty is there in conceiving the possibility
of delusions of the sense of hearing, such as we find
in this play. Music floating in the air, the musi-
cians being concealed, is no uncommon source of
surprise and pleasure even now. The art of the
ventriloquist may explain the rest.

But delusions of the sense of taste and of the
cravings of the appetite, it seems more difficult to
receive.

Yet Shakespeare had the best authorities for this:

" Erasmus reports a pretty piece of magic performed by a
Roman priest, that invited a company of ladies to a banquet, bidding them bring good stomachs with them. The ladies came, were
welcomed by him, entertained with delicate music, and were seated
at last at a table, according to their births. There were such variety
of rare and strange dishes, that they thought that others, not their
own nation, did furnish their table : they eat well, drank well,
and were merry ; and, which is better than a piece of cheese,
pippins or carroways to close up the mouth of the stomach after
supper, they were all welcome. When this feast, rather this fast,
was ended, and (which is not very usual with courtiers) grace
being said, they rendered the priest hearty thanks for their banquet, and went home. But they had not been there, at the most,
half an hour, but their stomachs began to call upon them for
meat ; for they were all as hungry as if they had eaten nothing
at the banquet, therefore did much wonder at themselves that
they should have such a great desire to meat, seeing they did but
newly come from such a royal entertainment. But this quaint
delusion the priest afterwards revealed to them, for although he
invited them to a feast, yet they had never a bit of meat, for his
art did delude both the eye that thought it saw such things, and
the palate that seemed to taste those delicates."—*Melton's Astrologaster*, 4to. 1620. P. 75.

A second instance is from Beard's *Theatre of God's Judgments*, 4to. 1631 :—" It was a common report that when any
gentlemen or lords came to see the Lord of Orne, they were entertained, as they thought, very honourably, being served with all

sort of most dainty fare and exquisite dishes, as if he had not spared to make them the best cheer that might be; but at their departure they that thought themselves well refreshed, found their stomachs empty, and almost pined for want of food, having neither eaten nor drunk anything save in imagination only, and it is to be thought their horses found no better fare than their masters." P. 121.

I have quoted these passages at length, as being curious in themselves, and as leading also to this remark, that Shakespeare has shewn his accustomed good sense by representing the banquet as only shewn to the king and his followers, not partaken of by them; thus removing this part of the operations of Prospero out of the scope of the *Incredulus odi*. I have no pleasure in repeating that such and such eminent commmentator is mistaken; but I cannot forbear adding that the note of Steevens (the only one in the Variorum) misleads, as he entirely mistakes the *kind* of illusion which Prospero, by his magic art, practised on the strangers.

For the honour of Shakespeare, it may also be observed, that when he introduces Ariel in the form of a harpy, at the disappearance of the banquet, there is not the smallest reason to suppose that he resorted to Phaer's Virgil for the attributes and doings of the harpies, but that he wrote the lines given to Ariel, in which we trace his familiarity with what we find in Virgil concerning them, from his own long laid-up recollections of the passage. It will be observed, that while he alludes to the invulnerability of the harpies, there is not the slightest verbal conformity with Phaer.

He evidently recollected the prophetic speech of Celeno, when he made Ariel speak at so great length, and in a style so different from the usual manner of that airy and sylph-like spirit.

VII.

PHILOLOGICAL REMARKS—RESTORATIONS—
CONCLUSION.

NO small portion of the legitimate criticism on these plays consists in the explanation of words or phrases which have disappeared from the language, or have lost the senses in which Shakespeare uses them. Much has been done, and done well in this department. It is easy to flout a commentator who explains a word which another may think needs no explanation : but in general, the assistance they give in this department is judicious, and many are the passages which would not be understood, but for the explanation which they have given of some obsolete word which occurs in them.

In *The Tempest*, are several words and phrases, in which most readers would require assistance. Such are the nautical phrases, and such are the words, *trash, hint, deck, coil, vast of night, dowl, candied, foyson, scamels, forth-right, pionied, twilled, rack*. Some of these are among the ἅπαξ λεγόμενα of the language.

Senses may undoubtedly be given to most of the passages in which these words occur, by readers who have not paid much attention to the language. But this is not the way in which a great author ought to be read.

For my own part, I beg to profess that I owe very much to the commentators ; and it is only in respect of a very few of these words that I would offer the following supplementary remarks.

TRASH.   *Act* i. *Sc.* 2.

" Being once perfected how to grant suits
How to deny them ; whom to advance, and whom
To *trash* for over-topping."

The figure is unquestionably one of *field-sports*, not of *gardening*. To *trash* a hound, is to place round his neck a collar weighted with lead. This is done when the huntsman wishes to restrain an eager hound, and to keep him back in a line with the rest of the pack.   Hawks were also *trashed :*

" So as they may be well compared to the ostrich, who (as the natural historian reports) hath the wings of an eagle, but never mounts ; so these have the eagle-wings of contemplation, being endued with the intellectual faculties of a reasonable soul, yet, either entangled with light chesses of vanity, or *trashed with checkered poizes* of self-conceit and singularity, they never mount above the verge of sensual pleasure."—*The English Gentleman*, by Richard Braithwaite, 4to. 1638, Epistle Dedicatory.

SCAMELS.   *Act* ii. *Sc.* 2.

" I'll bring thee
To clustering filberds ; and sometimes I'll get thee
Young *scamels* from the rock."

If this word is genuine, it is, as far as is known, peculiar to Shakespeare.   I think it genuine for the two following reasons : first, the word as it stands gives us a very melodious line, especially when pronounced, as it might be, *shamels ;* a line quite in Shakespeare's manner, in whom nothing is more remarkable than the extreme delicacy of his ear, and, as a consequence, the exquisite melody of his lines,

K

whether verse or prose. Secondly, the difficulty
which there is of finding a word which the printer
may be supposed to have mistaken. *Sea-mells* is
put in its place by the modern editors ; but the first
syllable of this word being long, while in the other
it is short, a line easily pronounced is turned into
one of which the pronunciation is difficult. Again,
sea-mell itself wants justification ; *sea-mew* or *sea-
maw* being the proper term for the species of gull
which is intended by it. Further, *gathering* seems
to be the action intended by the expression, " Sometimes I'll get thee," which applies rather to plants
growing on the rock, than to birds which have built
their nests thereon. And, lastly, the connection with
filberds leads us to something in the vegetable, rather
than the animal kingdom.

If we must interfere with the original text, and
not wait in hope of what future research, or rather
accident, may do for us, I should be inclined to read
at once :

> " and sometimes I'll get thee
> Young *samphire* from the rock."

This was to be done only as an occasional and choicer
service. It was a service of danger :

> " half-way down
> Hangs one that gathers samphire ; dreadful trade !"

But on the whole, I should leave the passage as it is.

FORTH-RIGHT. *Act* iii. *Sc.* 3.

> " here's a maze, trod indeed
> Through *forth-rights* and meanders."

It would not be easy to find this word in any other
writer than Shakespeare, in whose *Troilus and Cressida* it again occurs :

" If you give way
Or hedge aside from the direct *forth-right.*"
Act iii. *Sc.* 3.

In both places it evidently means no more than
straight lines.

RACK.   *Act* iv. *Sc.* 1.

" Leave not a *rack* behind."

I do not mean to dispute the conclusion to which
the commentators have come, and in which they
have been ably supported by Tooke, that *rack*, not
wreck, or *wrack* as Shakespeare wrote and pronounced it, is the word intended : and that the idea
betokened by it is that of light faint clouds; but
only to suggest a difficulty which none of them, nor
has Tooke himself, attempted to remove.

The word *rack* is, I believe, never found with the
indefinite article.

If it should turn out that to say *a rack*, would be
as improper as to say *a welkin*, we should be thrown
back on the word *wrack*, which would not give a
very bad sense, though, perhaps, one not so elegant
as that which is afforded by the rarer word, *rack.*

And while upon this passage, I would just remark on Mr. Malone's parallelism of it with a passage in Sir William Alexander's *Darius*, and the
conclusion to which he comes, that Shakespeare is
here little better than a copyist of an older poet ; that
the removal of the composition of *The Tempest* from
1611 to 1596 establishes, that if there is, any obligation on either side, it was the Scottish poet who was
the borrower, the *Darius* having been first published
in 1603.   But passages resembling this are to be
found in the poetry of all nations.

GREEN-SOUR. *Act* v. *Sc.* 1.

" You demy-puppets, that
By moon-shine do the *green-sour* ringlets make,
Whereof the ewe not bites."

This compound has been invented by the modern editors, the old editions having no hyphen, and there is no attempt to justify it. Yet, I believe, no other instance of such a compound is to be collected from any other writer, and perhaps, not even an instance in which the second word enters thus into combination with any other. The *wine-sour* plum approaches the nearest to it, but this is probably a corruption of some other word ; it is said, of *Windsor*, but this I doubt.

Mr. Douce suggests *green-sward.*

I would propose :

" By moon-shine *on* the green sour ringlets make."

Or if we suppose *on* to be elided :

" By moon-shine d'on the green sour ringlets make."

But I should prefer the former, were it not too obvious.

The changes which are for ever taking place in a language still living, renders the occasional assistance of a commentator necessary to the understanding all writings of an early date. But that assistance is peculiarly called for in respect of these writings, in preparing a text which is correct. Unfortunately, the plays of Shakespeare were not printed under the eye of the author, so that we in no case possess an authoritative impress, having the words, the points, the paragraphing, the capitals, and the italics, as he would have given them. It must also be admitted by every one, whatever his reverence may be for first folio, second folio, or the quartos, that all the old copies are printed in a very careless manner, and are full of very gross corruptions. Rowe was the first editor who undertook to revise the text, and give a text carefully printed, and as near as could be found to the text as intended by the author. But Rowe's principles of restoration were of the most arbitrary kind : he had very slight acquaintance with the language of Shakespeare's time, and still less with the contemporary writers, and he had the benefit of very few of the original copies. The consequence is, that Rowe's text is, in reality, very far from being that of the author : and all the subsequent texts have been more or less affected with his sophistications, though the profession has often been made of recourse being had to the old and original copies.

A person coming now with the intention of offering new illustrations, has therefore, in this department, two duties to perform : he has to bring back the received text to the original text, where it seems to him necessary to do so ; and he has to amend the original text itself, when it seems to him that there has been error from the beginning.

You will perceive at once that it would be absurd to attempt this in any book of annotation. Lying as it often does in the mere substitution of a comma for a colon, to do this with an explanation of eight or ten lines would be ridiculous. It can only be done when the text is printed entire ; a revised text of a revised edition, in which these minute changes might be silently made. Nevertheless, to shew that much remains to be done in this department, I shall take

a *single scene* of this play, and, with the old copies
before me, shew what changes I should propose to
make in the text to bring it back to what seems to
me to be the genuine text of the author. The scene
is the second of the first act :

> " *Prospero.* The direful spectacle of the *wreck*, which touch'd
>   The very virtue of compassion in thee,
>   I have with such *provision* in mine art," &c.

Shakespeare wrote *wrack*, and the ear perceives at
once that something is lost in melody by the substitution of *wreck*. This uncalled-for change has been
made throughout the play, and I believe in every
other place in which the word occurs ; yet, that much
is lost in melody will be apparent to every one who
will repeat aloud the two following lines of this play,
with the word *wrack* and the word *wreck*.

> " Weeping again, the king my father's wrack (*wreck*)."

> " Supposing that he saw the king's ship wrack'd (*wreck'd*)."

The cause of the difference is, that by pronouncing
the preceding words, the organs of speech are put
into a more favourable position for pronouncing
wrack than *wreck;* and the organs of hearing are
put into a more favourable condition for receiving
with pleasure the fuller sound of *wrack*. These are
but niceties, but poetry is a luxury, and should therefore be as refined and perfect as possible.

The reason for the substitution is evident. *Wrack*
has in a great measure gone out of use, though we
still use the familiar phrase " wrack and ruin." But
wrack continued in use long after the time of Shakespeare, and cannot have been, by any means, extinct
in the days of Rowe.

What could editors, who proceed upon principles which lead to such a substitution, do with this couplet of the *Lucrece*:

" O, this dread night, would'st thou one hour come back
I could prevent this storm, and shun thy *wrack* ?"

But enough.*

There is another word in this passage about which some doubt may be entertained, *Provision*. This is the reading of the first folio, but it may be questioned whether it ought not to be *Prevision*. The second folio has in this place *Compassion*, which is one of the many gross and palpable errors of the press, a word of the preceding line repeated.

I cannot forbear to quote a passage from the *Modern Policies*, a work full of admirable political wisdom, attributed to Sancroft, of which the fifth edition was published in 1654, as affording some countenance to the reading of *prevision*: and the

---

* Yet, let me shew the effect of this principle of editorial labour, which is in fact nothing less than the periodical adjusting the writings of a great poet to the changes which are ever silently taking place in a language still living, in two other instances from another play.

What can be more inharmonious than the following line ?

" That now is lying in Marseilles'. road."
TAMING OF THE SHREW, ii. 1.

But is Shakespeare guilty of it ?   No.   See what he wrote:

" That now is lying in Marsellis road."

Which was, no doubt, the approved pronunciation of the time.

Again, in the same play :

" I am arrived from fruitful Lombardy."

So we must now read ; but Shakespeare suggests another and a better sound :

" I am arrived from fruitful Lumbardy."

rather, because there occurs in it a phrase which may
serve to justify a few words in the first scene, which
appear to need justification : " You do assist the
storm."

" We allow the disburthening of a ship in imminent peril of
wrack; but this will not excuse those who, upon a fond or feigned
prevision of a state-*tempest*, shall immediately cast law and conscience overboard, discard and quit rudder and steerage, and thus
assist the danger they pretend to fear."

Must he not have remembered Shakespeare's *Tempest* when he wrote the passage?

> " *Prospero.* By what? by any other house or person ?
> Of any thing the image tell me, that
> Hath kept with thy remembrance."

Thus the passage is exhibited. In the first folio it
stands thus :

> " By what? by any other house, or person?
> Of any thing the image, tell me, that
> Hath kept with thy remembrance."

And this appears to me to represent much more justly
the pauses which Shakespeare meant to occur, and generally the manner in which the words should be read
or spoken so as to express what he designed to convey.
Dramatic language, even in the most sustained parts,
has something of the colloquial, but in passages not
sustained, of which this is one, the colloquial style
will be every where apparent. It will be somewhat
abrupt, always easy, the reverse of the *set phrase*,
such as we find in oratorical and other composition.
Besides, the speaking sententiously, abruptly, with
the air of one who had found less use for language
than those who have lived in constant intercourse
with many beings like themselves, and sometimes as

a person deeply reflective, belongs to the character of Prospero.

The instances are numerous in which the modern editors have overlooked the colloquial character of dramatic writing, and given us, instead of the natural easy language of Shakespeare, their own set and stiff phrases, out of a design to make every sentence uttered complete, or every line of verse conformable to their notions of his prosody. The very first speech in *As You Like It*, is a very memorable instance of the fault I mean to point out.

" *Prospero.* If thou remember'st aught, ere thou cam'st here,
      How thou cam'st here thou may'st."

Strike out the intrusive comma after *aught;* it is not in the original, and obscures the meaning.

" *Prospero.* Twelve *years* since, Miranda, twelve *years* since."

Thus all the modern copies, and Mr. Steevens goes so far as to tell us, that the first *years* is to be read as a dissyllable! But see the reading of the old copies :

" Twelve *year* since, Miranda, twelve *year* since."

A line which satisfies the ear, and is, without doubt, what Shakespeare intended. I need not tell you that one of the commonest idioms of the language which he used is a substantive of time, weight, distance, or money in the singular form, though many are spoken of. See, for example, " a twelve month," " a hundred pound," and many other well-known phrases.

" *Prospero.* Thy mother was a piece of virtue, and
      She said—thou wast my daughter; and thy father
      Was Duke of Milan; and his only heir
      A princess ;—no worse issued."

A has been substituted for *And,* the original reading.
Some of the less critical editions have bolder de-
partures from the original text. Yet that text needs
little correction. I should print it thus :

> " Thy mother was a piece of virtue, and
> She said thou wast my daughter ; and thy father
> Was Duke of Milan :—and [thou] his only heir—
> And princess—no worse issued."

He unfolds to her by degrees what she was, his
language having all the ease of actual conversation :
(1) his daughter ; (2) daughter to the Duke of Milan ;
(3) sole heir to the duchy; and (4) the word so
pleasing to a lady's ear, a princess, spoken with a
pause before the word. I add *thou*, inclosed in
crotchets, not that I think the passage really needs
it.

> " *Miranda.*   O, my heart bleeds
> To think *o' the* teen that I have turn'd you to."

A question might be raised on the propriety of retaining contracts such as these at all, and whether
the words should not be printed in full, leaving the
reader or the speaker to contract them at his pleasure.
But if *of* is to become *o'*, *the* should become *th'*, as
in the original editions. We have the injudicious
substitution of *further* for *farther* in this speech :

> " *Prospero* My brother and thy uncle, call'd *Antonio.*"

This is another instance of a slight deterioration of
Shakespeare's exquisite melody by a useless alteration. A nice ear will be sensible at once that something is lost.

> " My brother and thy uncle call'd *Anthonio.*"

But how much better Shakespeare knew what to write than his editors, will be more evident by another passage, in which the same unwise alteration has been made :

> "   ~~whereon~~
> A treacherous army levied, one mid-night (midnight)
> Fated to th' purpose, did Anthonio open
> The gates of Milan."

> " *Prospero*.   As, at that time,
> *Through* all the signories it was the first,
> And Prospero the prime duke ; being so reputed
> In dignity, and, for the liberal arts
> Without a parallel ; these being all my study,
> The government I cast upon my brother,
> And to my state grew stranger."

The word *through*, which does indeed give a kind of sense, is the reading of the first folio, corrected in the second to *though*. I regard this as one of the many valuable improvements of that edition, not an editorial conjecture, but a reading proceeding from the same authority which gave us *through* in the first edition, which preceded the second only nine years. I have before alluded to this passage, and shewn what Shakespeare evidently intended to express, namely, that the Duchy of Milan took precedence among the several duchies of Europe.

Though, however, is to be read with a syllable after it, which is elided, just as in another passage of this scene we have *but* for *but the*, or rather *but th'*, and *with* for *with the*, or *with th'*.* The word elided is *of*, or thus, *Though 'f.*

---

* There are other instances in this play of the kind of elision here spoken of; and I shall annex them, partly to support the

We have thus a complete and consecutive sentence, though, like the rest, broken and colloquial: "Though Milan was accounted the first of the great seignories,† and Prospero prime duke in Europe (having the general reputation and allowance of this precedence and dignity), and had also the higher reputation for the liberal arts; I neglected the affairs of state, threw the government on my brother, and devoted myself entirely to those studies." On the whole, the passage may be regulated thus:

> " As, at that time,
> Though [of] all the seignories it was the first,
> And Prospero the prime duke; (being so reputed
> In dignity ;) and for the liberal arts
> Without a parallel.—These being all my study,
> The government I cast upon my brother,
> And to my state grew stranger."

> " *Prospero.*   Confederates
> (So dry he was for sway) *with the* King of Naples

---

new reading I have proposed of this passage, and partly as suggesting other restorations of the existing text :

> " Had I [the] plantation of this isle."   *Act* ii. *Sc.* 1.

> " I am more serious than my custom: you
> Must be so too if [ye] heed me."   *Act* ii. *Sc.* 1.

> " My dukedom since you have given [it] me again."
>   *Act* v. *Sc.* 1.

> " We were dead on sleep,
> And (how we know not) all clapp'd under [the] hatches."
>   *Act* v. *Sc.* 1.

> " Which (part of it) I'll waste
> With such discourse, as, I not doubt, shall make [it]
> Go quick away."   *Act* v. *Sc.* 1.

† The word *Seignory* denoted any sovereignty, regal or ducal : Thus, " Of all the Seignories of the world, the realm of England is the country where the commonwealth is best governed, the people least oppressed :" *Comines,* b. v. c. 18, as quoted in Nash's *Quaternio,* 4to, 1636, p. 67.

To give him annual tribute, do him homage;
Subject his coronet to his crown, and bend
The dukedom yet unbow'd, (alas, poor Milan!)
To *most* ignoble stooping."

To maintain uniformity, it should be printed thus:
with'. The old copies have no *the*. In the last line
most is an unauthorised substitution for *much*, the
reading of the old copies.

" *Prospero*. A treacherous army levied, one midnight."

Here the blank verse halts; but of its lameness
Shakespeare is guiltless. See what he wrote:

" A treacherous army levied, one mid-night."

" *Miranda*.   Wherefore did they not
    That hour destroy us?
Prospero.   Well demanded, wench:
    My tale provokes that question. Dear, they durst not;
    (So dear the love my people bore me), nor set
    A mark so bloody on the business; but
    With colours fairer painted their foul ends."

This is the reading of the modern copies, but is not
the reading of those which are authoritative. The
difference is not great; but as long as Shakespeare is
what he is, we must desire to possess what he himself has given us. What he really wrote was this:

                    " Dear, they durst not,
    So dear the love my people ̄bore me : nor set
    A mark so bloody on the business; but
    With colours fairer, painted their foul ends."

" Nor set," being, " Nor did they set." Some may
think the reading of the editor's the better. Be it
so; but that is not the question in editorial labour.

> " *Prospero.* In few they hurried us aboard a bark :
> Bore us some leagues to sea; where they prepar'd
> A rotten carcase of a *boat*, not rigg'd,
> Nor tackle, sail nor mast ; the very rats
> Instinctively *had* quit it."

This is an editorial text, open in three points to question. I ought not to say this of one of them, for who will think that the substitution of *had* for *have*, which is the reading of the old copies, has any other effect than to injure the spirit of the passage? Prospero was making the past present. The second folio reads :

> " A rotten carcase of a Butt, not rigg'd,
> Nor tackle, nor sail, nor mast ; the very rats
> Instinctively have quit it."

Where the second *nor* is added to the reading of the first, to the improvement of the spirit. The great critical canon of the *Durior Lectio præferenda*, which ought to be always present when we are employed on ascertaining the true text of Shakespeare, would lead us to retain the word *Butt*, which is printed in both the first and second folios with a capital letter, and can hardly be what the modern editors have regarded it, a mere misprint for the word *Boat*. A large wine-butt cut transversely might make a kind of boat carrying a little food, robes and books, and one person with a young child, about whose lives those who committed them to the sea were not in the least solicitous, and perhaps meant to drown them. At all events, it is a reading which comes to us with the weight of the authority of both the first and second folios, and deserves consideration. Nor is the incident so very unlike the manner of the romance writers at the revival of letters : beside, Prospero was an enchanter, who could control the elements. Should the story on which Shakespeare constructed his plot ever be discovered, I should expect to find that to such a frail bark Prospero and his lovely charge were committed. Were I, however, fully satisfied that it is the genuine reading, I should not hesitate to say that the incident was no invention of Shakespeare, and regard it as an additional proof that he was working on an original.

> " *Prospero.* By providence divine."

The period is an insertion of the modern editors. The folios have a comma only, and this no doubt was what Shakespeare intended.

> " *Prospero.*   and here
> Have I, thy schoolmaster, made thee more profit
> Than other *princes* can," &c.

The folios have *princesse*, which I regard as on the whole the better reading.

> " *Ariel.*   The fire, and cracks
> Of sulphurous roaring, the most mighty Neptune
> *Seem'd* to besiege, and make his bold waves tremble,
> Yea, his dread trident shake."

Why *seem'd*, when Shakespeare wrote *seem?* Another instance of his intention to realize the scene, by making the past present, defeated by the intermeddling of injudicious editors. But the effect of the substitution does not end here: the spirit of the succeeding clause is greatly weakened by turning the words *make* and *shake* into infinitives. In labour like this, one feels sometimes as he does who sees a fine picture spoiled by the mending of an inferior artist, or an ancient inscription ruined by bungling attempts to restore it.

> " *Ariel.*   All, *but* mariners."

So all the copies, old and new : but the word *but* should be read thus, *but'*, as *with'* in a former instance, the word *the* being elided after it. To be consistent with themselves, the modern editors should have printed it thus : " All but the mariners."

> " *Ariel. Whom*, with a charm join'd to their suffer'd labour
>   I have left asleep."

What we call the rules of grammar are nothing more than abstracts of the usage of the best writers and speakers. Now, in the time of Shakespeare, the best writers would not scruple to write or speak *who* in this grammatical construction, as Shakespeare in the genuine copies has done. And that Shakespeare wrote *who* and *whom* indifferently, is evident from the testimony of the original copies, and even from the far greater beauty of this line as he gave it; to say nothing of what was the license or usage of the time. A little above he has " Whom I left," where the word is followed by a vowel.

> " *Prospero.* Go, make thyself like a nymph of the sea; be
>   subject
>   To no sight but thine and mine."

Why refuse the reading of the second folio :

> " Go, make thyself like to a nymph o' th' sea ?"

A more melodious line. In some of the modern edi-
tions, the words " thine and" have been omitted, but
I am glad to see them restored in the latest of the
Variorums.

> " *Prospero.* Come, thou tortoise ! when ? "

Steevens inserted the word *forth* after *come*, which
gives the line a better cadence : only let it be placed
in crotchets, as wanting the authority of the old
copies.   Mr. Malone repudiates it.

> " *Prospero.*   thou shalt be pinch'd
>   As thick as *honey-combs*, each pinch more stinging
>   Than bees that made them."

A corrupted taste, or an ignorance of the idioms of
the language in which Shakespeare wrote, and indeed, I may say, of idiomatic and ordinary English
in the present day, has given us the word printed in
italics, while the original has *honey-comb*.   How
much more glibly, how much more Shakesperian,
the line reads.   It is evident for what reason the
modern editors have made the change.   It was to
satisfy a supposed necessity created by the plural
pronoun *them*.   But Shakespeare had not, in his
intention, a number of honey-combs, but the cells in
a single honey-comb.   " As thick as honey-comb,"
as thick as lie the cells in a honey-comb.   It is perhaps to refine too much to represent Shakespeare as
attentive at the moment to their hexagonal form, by
which the greatest possible number are crowded into
a given space.

> " *Caliban.* Curs'd be 1 that did so."

L

Thus, Malone, and some other modern editors, after
the first folio, refusing again the better reading of
the second :

> " Curs'd be I that I did so."

> " *Ferdinand.*   My prime request
> Which I do last pronounce, is, O you wonder!
> If you be *made*, or no ?
>
> *Miranda.*   No wonder, Sir,
> But certainly a maid."

Here is an instance of another kind : first, second,
and third folios read *maid;* but because in the fourth
(an edition of no more authority in the question
of the text than Rowe's, or any other) is found
made, which was probably only a misprint, we must
have this reading obtruded upon us : poor, weak,
and in every point of view worse than that of the
earlier folios, which have *maid*. If Shakespeare had
meant that Ferdinand should ask if Miranda were
a created being or a goddess, would he have put the
question in such a poor manner as this ? I should
not pretend to vindicate the true reading as one of
Shakespeare's happiest efforts; but in all which passes
between Ferdinand and Miranda, we are to regard
them as under spells created by Prospero, and the
whole, from the first sight of each other to the be-
trothment, was to be concluded within six hours. The
passage which Farmer, one of the most efficient of
the commentators, has quoted from Lylly's Gallathea,
is a sufficient justification, if any were wanted : " The
question among men is common ; Are you a maid ?"
The remainder of this extremely pleasing scene
requires little emendation. But now, let me ask, if
in one scene there are at least ten passages in which

the text has suffered some deterioration, either in sense or melody, is it not manifest that something remains to be done before we can say that we fully enjoy " our beloved Shakespeare and what he hath left us."

Is not a minute examination of the text of this great author as worthy a work as similar critical labour bestowed on any dramatic writer of any nation and of any tongue ?

However, it is to be hoped that there are few scenes which were originally so carelessly printed as this, and which have been so unskilfully restored.

But I am sensible that this is not the place for this kind of very minute criticism : and even your patience, indomitable as it is when the subject is the writings of Shakespeare, may already have become wearied ; so that it is high time I bring this letter to a close.

I have indeed said nearly all that when I began to write it was in my mind to say ; and some things (especially in the notes) which I had then no intention of saying. You will have perceived that it was no part of my design to give a full and proper commentary on the play, but only to supply deficiencies and correct mistakes, when my own studies of these writings, and other reading and reflection of my own, enabled me to do so.

Whether you, or whether the public, deem me right or wrong in the conclusions to which I have been led, I now claim that it be allowed me that I have paid some attention to these writings, and that when I announced my *New Illustrations*, it was not with any design to get a fellowship in the cry of commentators, without having done something to deserve it.

Need I say that I have too great a respect for
you and for truth, not to be perfectly sincere in all
that I have written concerning this play. This is no
experiment upon public credulity, nor an attempt
at gaining the poor praise which is yielded to the
ingenious defender of improbable theories. If I am
wrong, my mistakes may serve as beacons to some
other adventurer in this sea of discovery. If I am
right, it is manifest that a great revolution will be
effected in the criticism of this play. Such kind of
revolution it is in my power to produce in the criticism of some other of these plays : and there is not
one in the whole collection on which I cannot throw
some new light, which, faint as in some instances it
may be, those who value Shakespeare as you do, or
who regard his name as "the greatest name in our
literature,—the greatest in all literature," as **Mr.**
Hallam has lately so emphatically expressed himself,
—would not think ought to be thrown upon them.

What discoveries I have made have been for the
most part the results of some little attention to the
language, literature, and transactions of the age
in which he lived; not the great political transactions so much, as those minor events which were
topics of the day, and on which it might be expected
that a dramatic writer such as Shakespeare, who had
his eyes every where, would seize : and for these I have
not been content to go to the printed literature of the
period only, for I have sometimes gone with success
to manuscripts in private hands or in public depo-
sitories, to what I may call the obscure and scarcely
accessible sources of historical knowledge.

Further discoveries it is not probable that I shall
make, for I have now to attend to other writings and

other kind of men, with few intervals for any thing merely recreative. And further, though I need not yet to take up the words of the poetical Lord Vaux, to which the use made of them by Shakespeare has given a celebrity they could not have asserted for themselves, and complain that

> " Age with his stealing steps
> Hath claw'd me in his clutch :"

yet it is time I should consider (when ought it not to be considered ?) how many glasses may be yet to run, and remember what the hand findeth to do, to do it.

These were the considerations which determined me, some time ago, to put into form what I had collected, and to entertain the design of adding it to the heap of Shakespeare criticism, made *publici juris* by the press. Perhaps I was wrong : the present may not be a time favourable to the production of works of exact literature and minute criticism. But whether this letter be my only contribution to that peculiar literature which Shakespeare has created, and my *New Illustrations*, instead of finding a place in the libraries of those who love this species of literature, and delight in any thing that makes these writings more perfectly understood, will remain to perplex my executors, and to be placed at last in my inventory as " a bundle of written papers, value nil," it will never repent me that I have spent many hours which might perhaps otherwise have been passed in recreations which tended to no useful purpose, in attention to these writings, and the means by which they might be illustrated. My labours, if labours they are to be called, when they have been in reality but a

laborum dulce lenimen, have been " innocent at least,
if not ingenuous," as you may remember a learned
and amiable prelate remarks of very similar labours
of his own. I might follow him further, and say with
truth, that I have delighted in them the more because
they have so often formed the subject of much
pleasing communication with you.

Before closing this epistle I must remark that I
have often regretted that so much respect has not
been paid to Dryden as to find a place in the prolegomena of this play for the portion of the prologue
to his own and Davenant's transversion of it, in which
he pays so fine a compliment to Shakespeare. Of
that transversion little is to be said in praise, though
in the parts which are added there are two very
beautiful passages. But the prologue is, so far,
worthy Dryden and Shakespeare. Collins' Dirge
has been exalted to the honours of a place in the
editions of *Cymbeline*. Moore's Cell of Ariel would
deserve the same honour, were Bermuda ever to
be restored to its old connection with this play : and
I confidently expect to see Mr. Tennyson's exquisite
poem, Mariana, subjoined to that, which is however
perhaps the least pleasing of all the plays, *Measure
for Measure*. Such supplements ought to be made
only in the case of very rare excellence. But surely
a place might have been found for lines in which
one great poet praises another, and in strains such
as these :

> As when a tree's cut down, the secret root
> Lives under ground, and thence new branches shoot :
> So from old Shakespeare's honour'd dust, this day
> Springs up and buds a new reviving play.
> Shakespeare, who (taught by none) did first impart
> To Fletcher wit, to labouring Jonson art.

He, monarch-like, gave those his subjects law,
And is that nature which they paint and draw.
Fletcher reach'd that which on his heights did grow,
Whilst Jonson crept and gathered all below ;
This did his love, and this his mirth digest :
One imitates him most, the other best.
If they have since out-writ all other men,
'Tis with the drops which fell from Shakespeare's pen.
The storm which vanish'd on the neighb'ring shore,
Was taught by Shakespeare's Tempest first to roar.
That innocence and beauty which did smile
In Fletcher, grew on this Enchanted Isle.
But Shakespeare's magic could not copy'd be ;
Within that circle none durst walk but he.
I must confess 'twas bold, nor would you now
That liberty to vulgar wits allow,
Which work by magic supernatural things :
But Shakespeare's pow'r is sacred as a king's.
Those legends from old priesthood were receiv'd,
And he then writ, as people then believ'd.

I am, my dear Sir,

Your truly faithful friend,

JOSEPH HUNTER.

To Benjamin Heywood Bright, Esq.
Nov. 29, 1839.

THE END.

C. Whittingham, Tooks Court, Chancery Lane, London.

CPSIA information can be obtained
at www.ICGtesting.com
Printed in the USA
BVOW09s1134031117

499468BV00026B/1315/P